Poly fusion

Coloring book

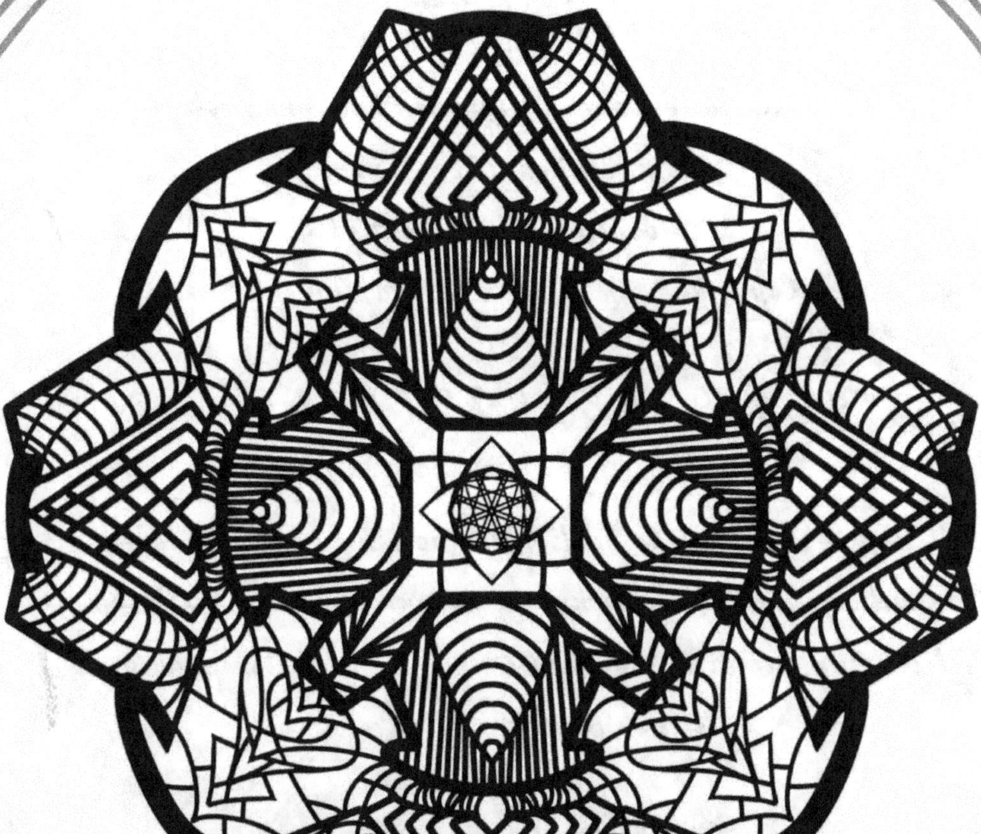

By Autumnzelinie

Published by

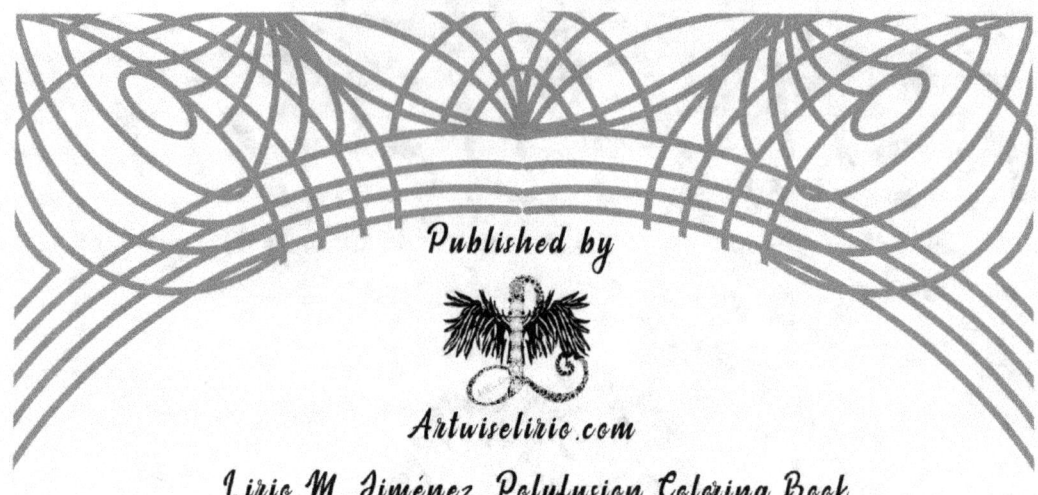

Artwiselirio.com

Lirio M. Jiménez, Polyfusion Coloring Book

1st published 2023 USA

Independantly Published

Copyright   2023, Lirio M. Jiménez

ISBN: 9 7 9 8 3 9 2 9 7 4 2 4 5

Publishers QR Code

https://linktr.ee/artwiselirio

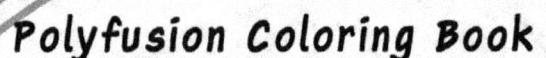

Polyfusion Coloring Book

In the 80's, I noticed the calming
effects that drawing and coloring
had for me when ever I had a
stressful event. Both my books,
as I have been coloring the
previous book, noticed that it had
the same calming effects as I get
when I create these intricate
patterns.
In hopes that you have a deeper
calming experience, I've created a
book completely of polygonal
mandalas for those that search
for inner peace.
You owe it to yourself, to break
from all your thoughts, wind down.
Happy people have healthy minds.
Sincerely,

Artwiselirio

I would like to thank my family for
all its support.

Art 2 heal Art 2 chill
All ages 13 and up.

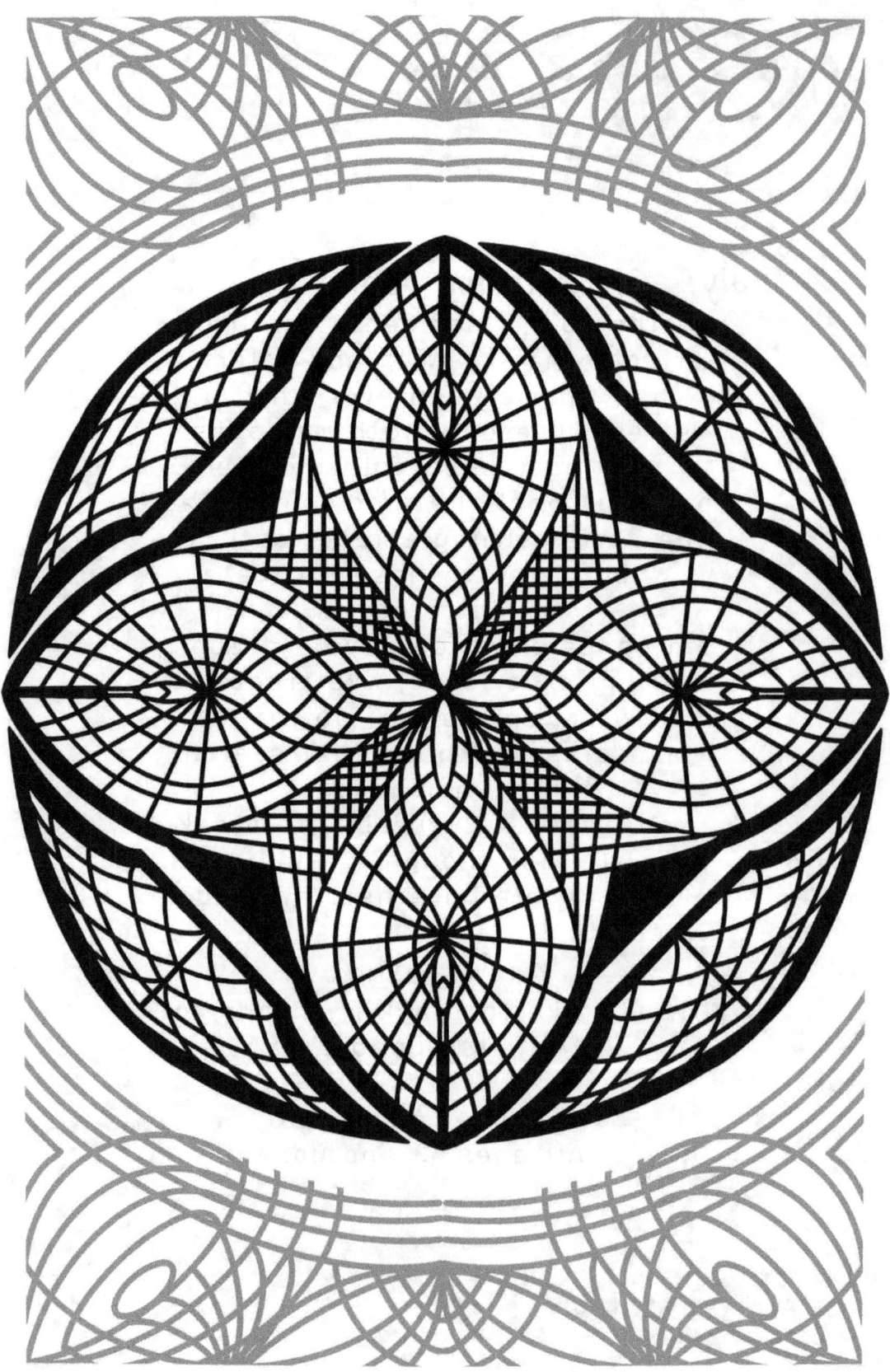

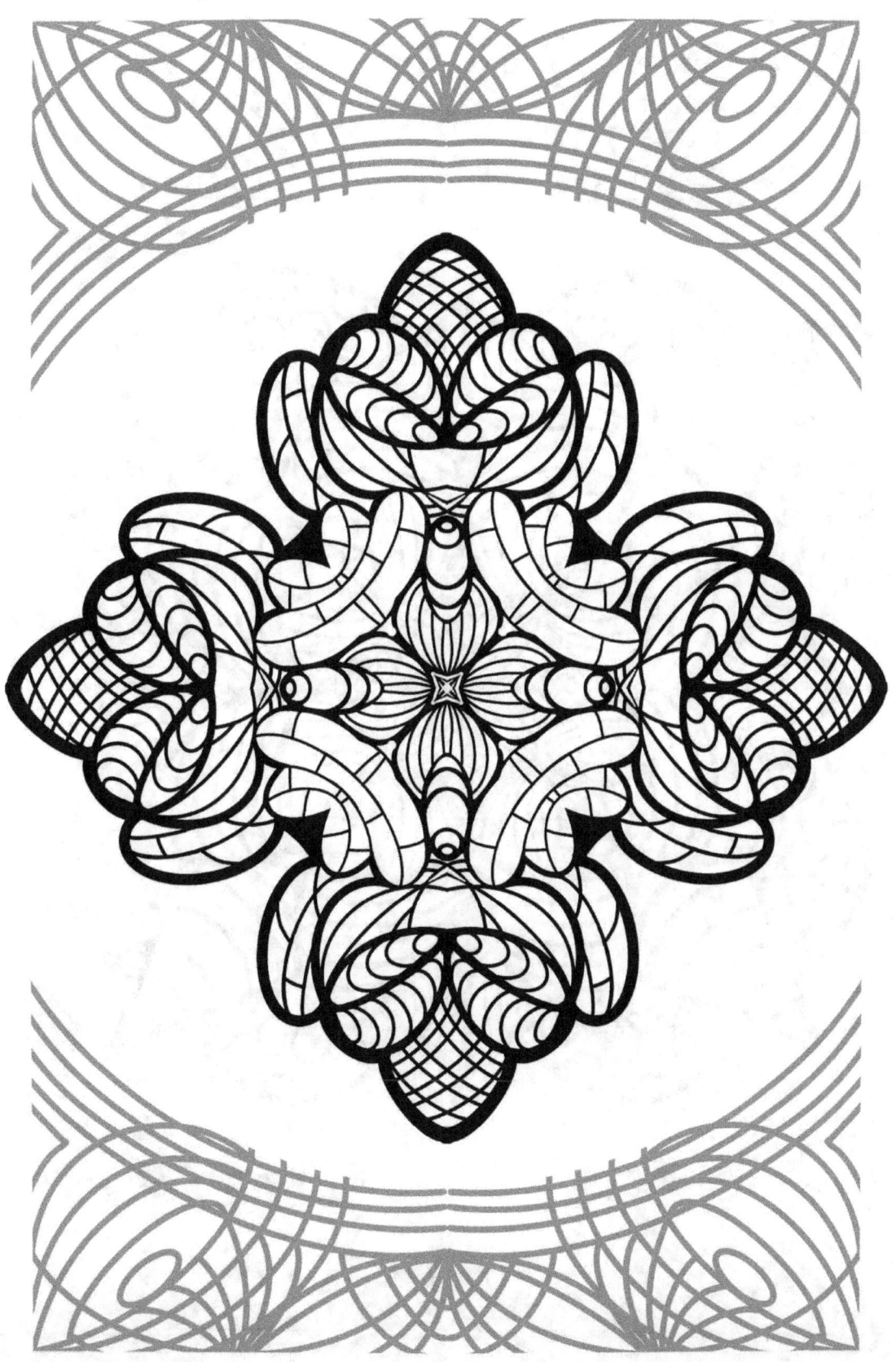

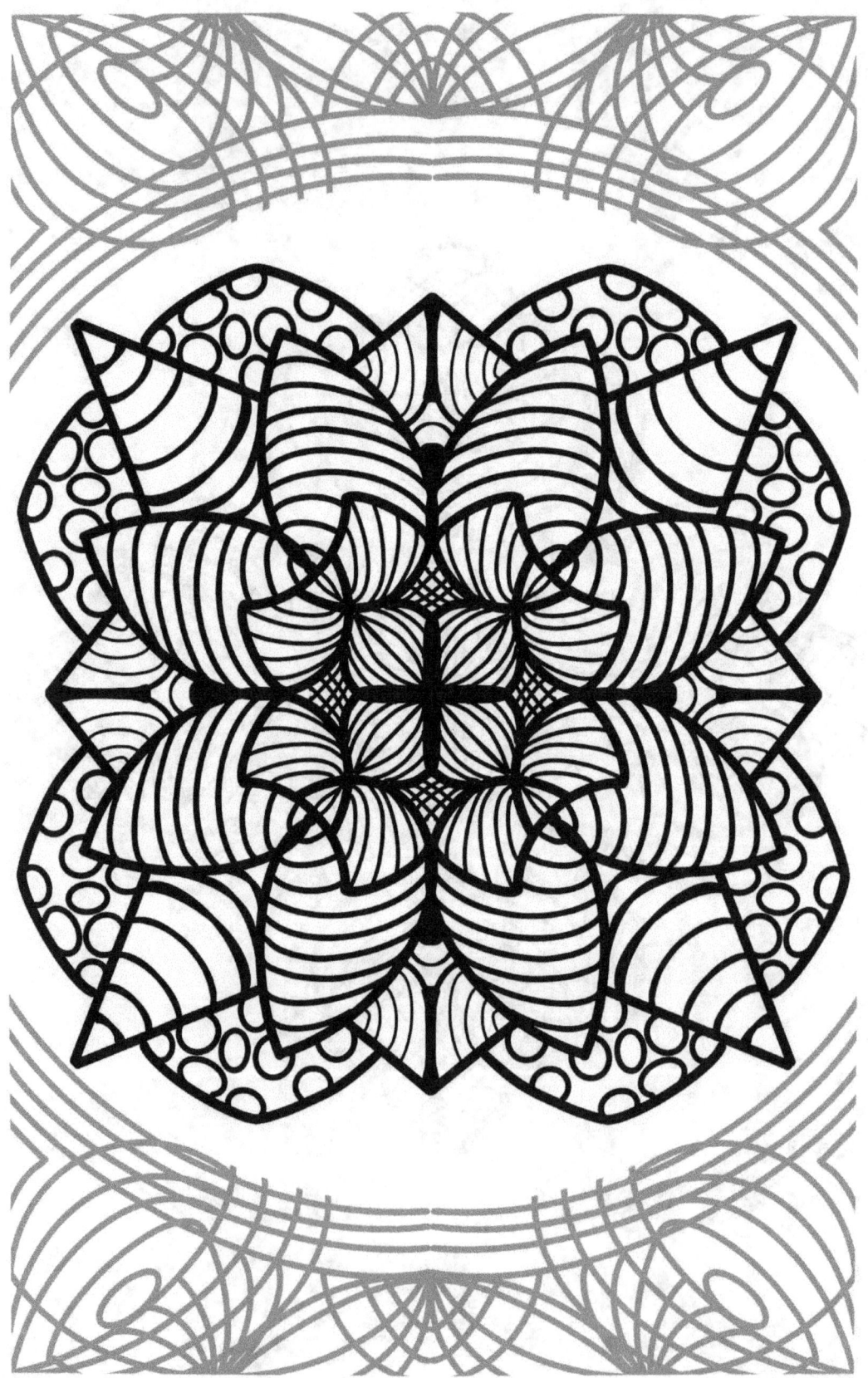

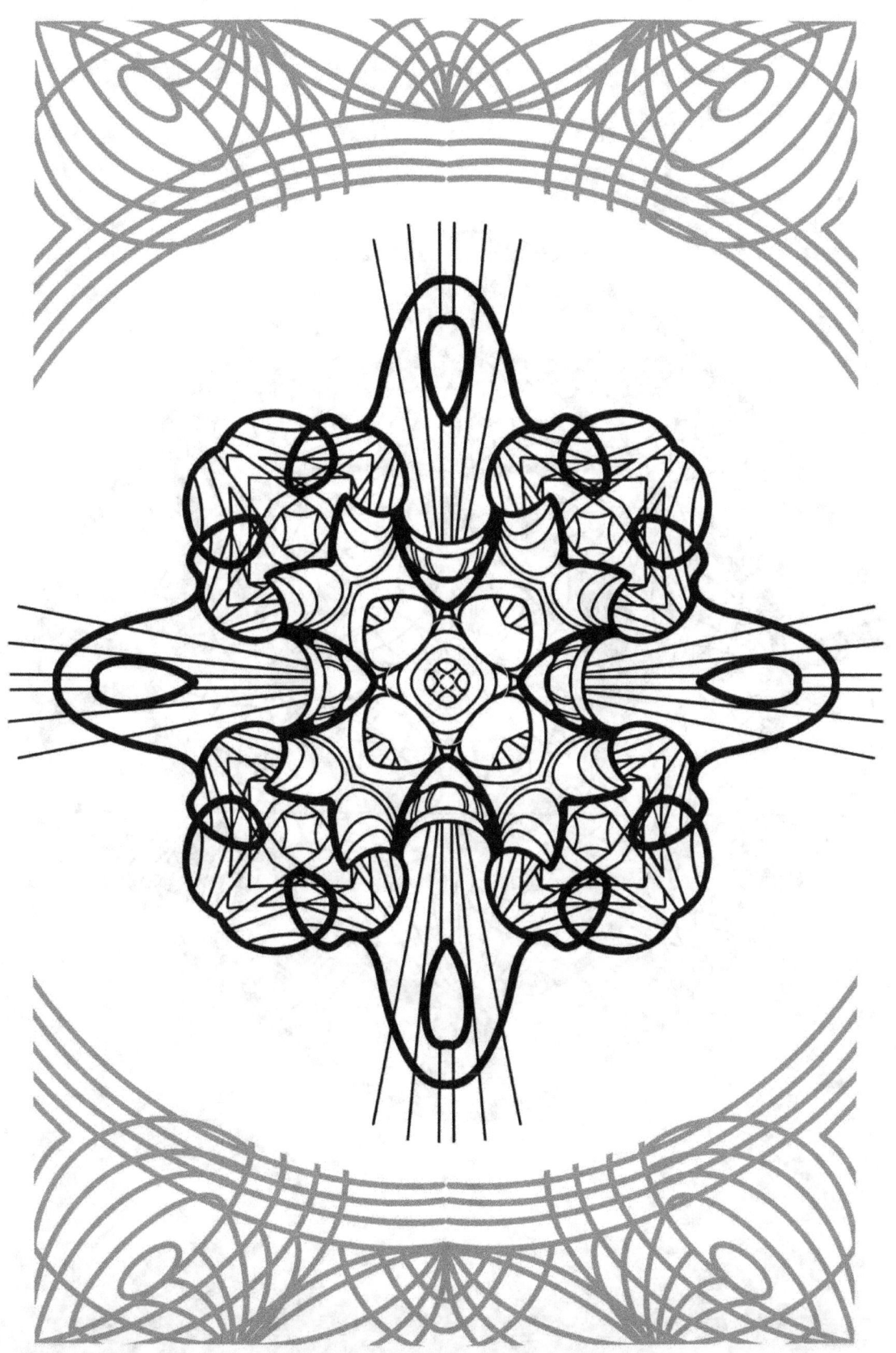

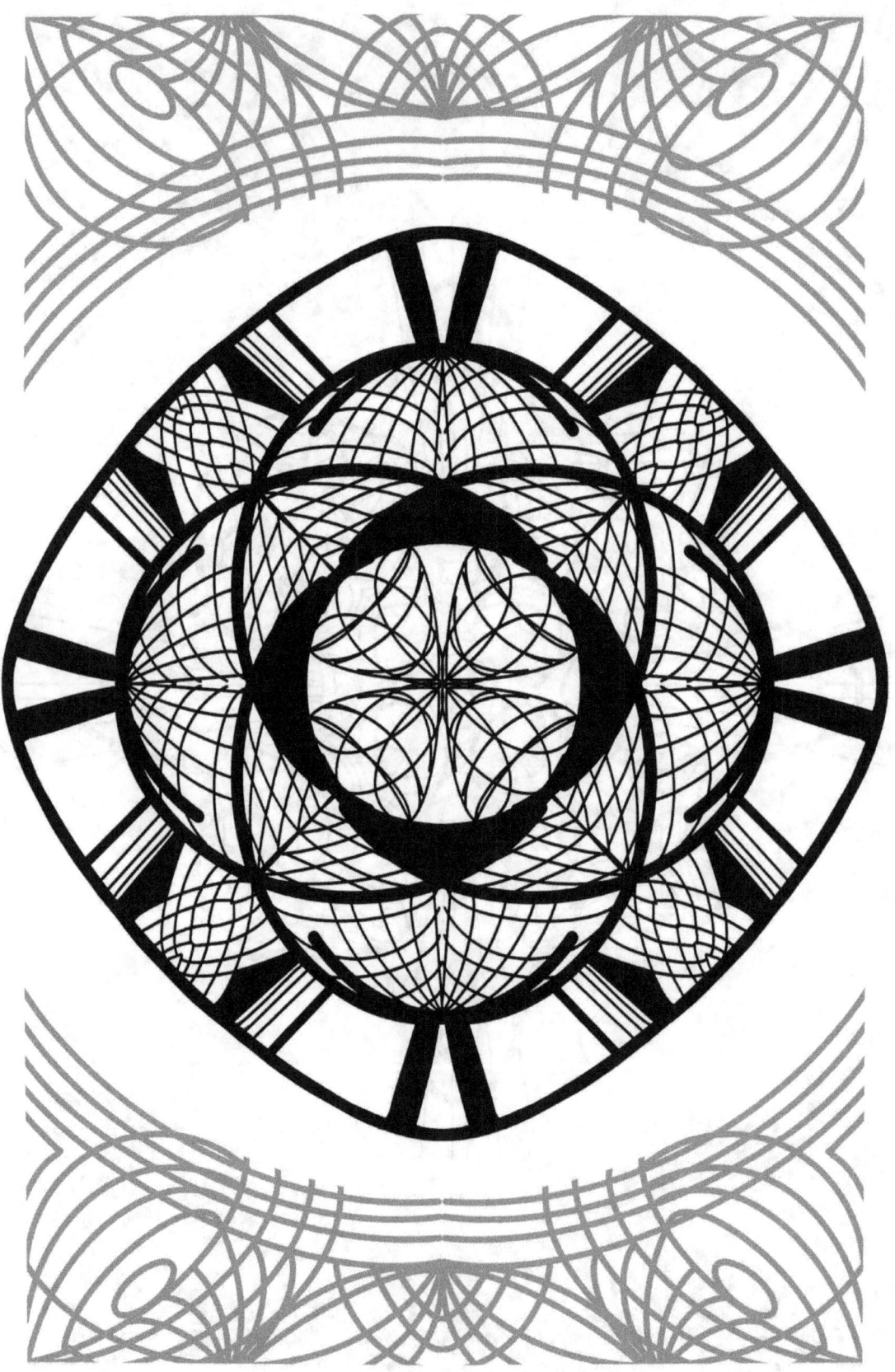

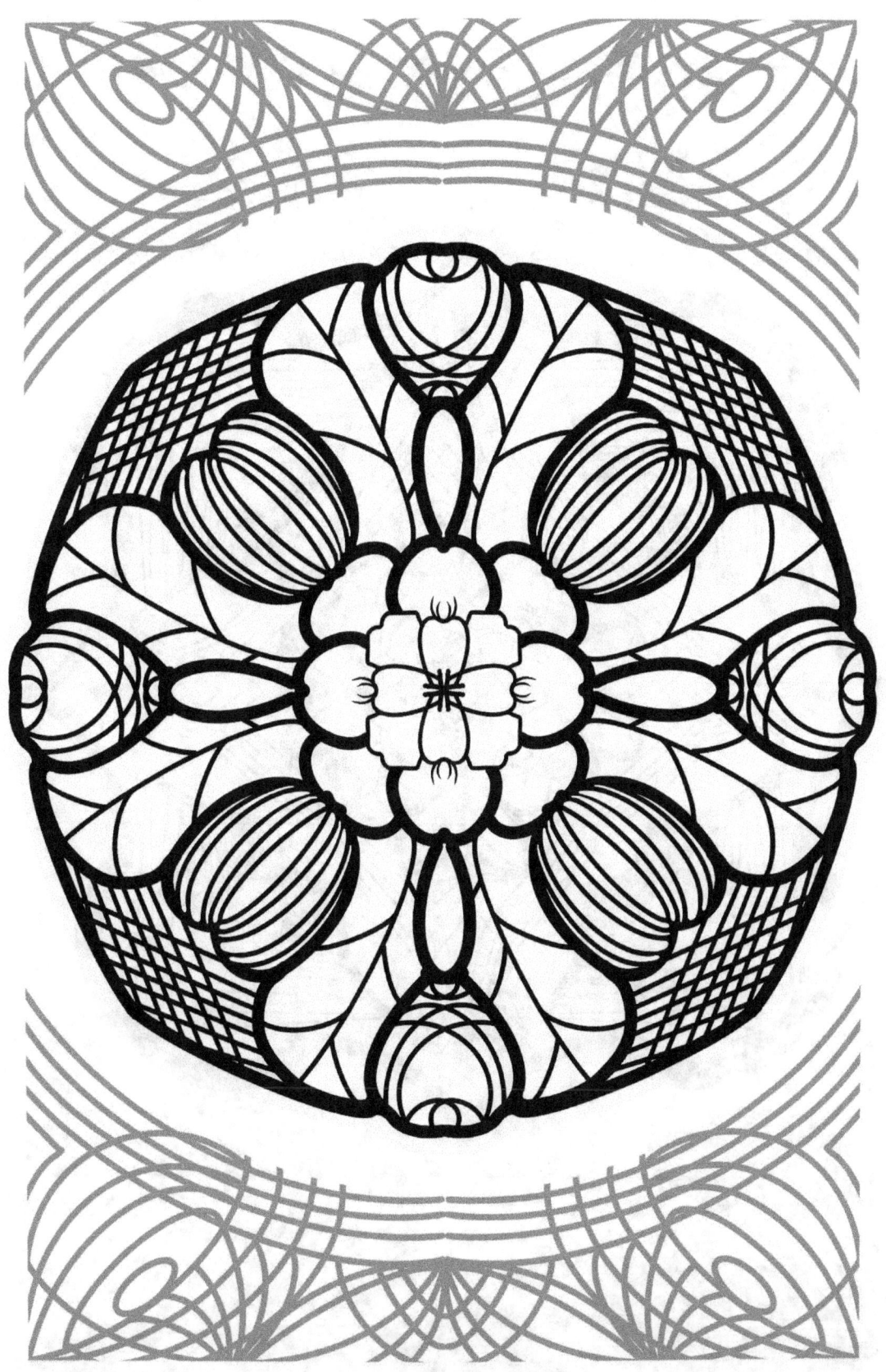

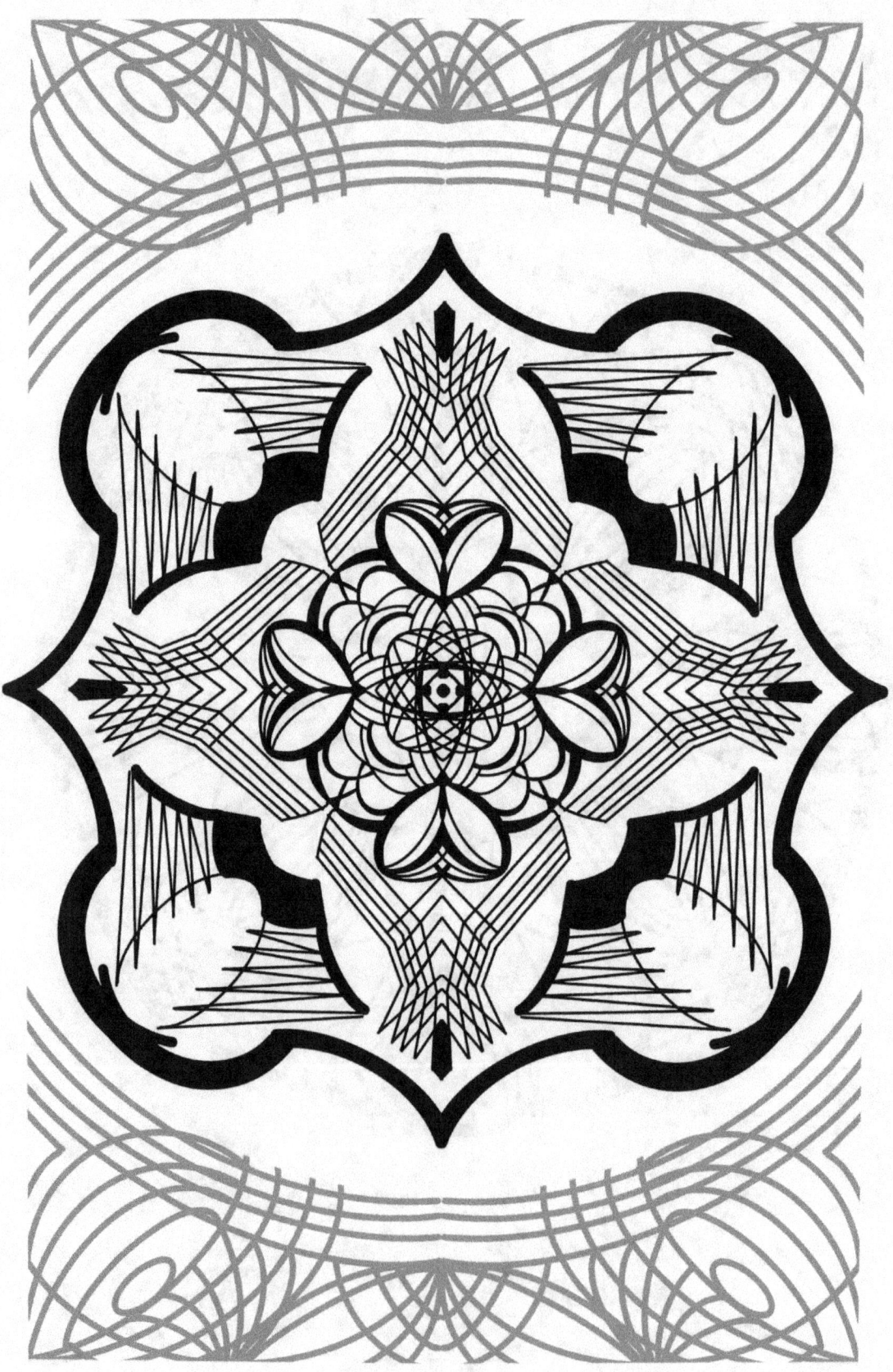

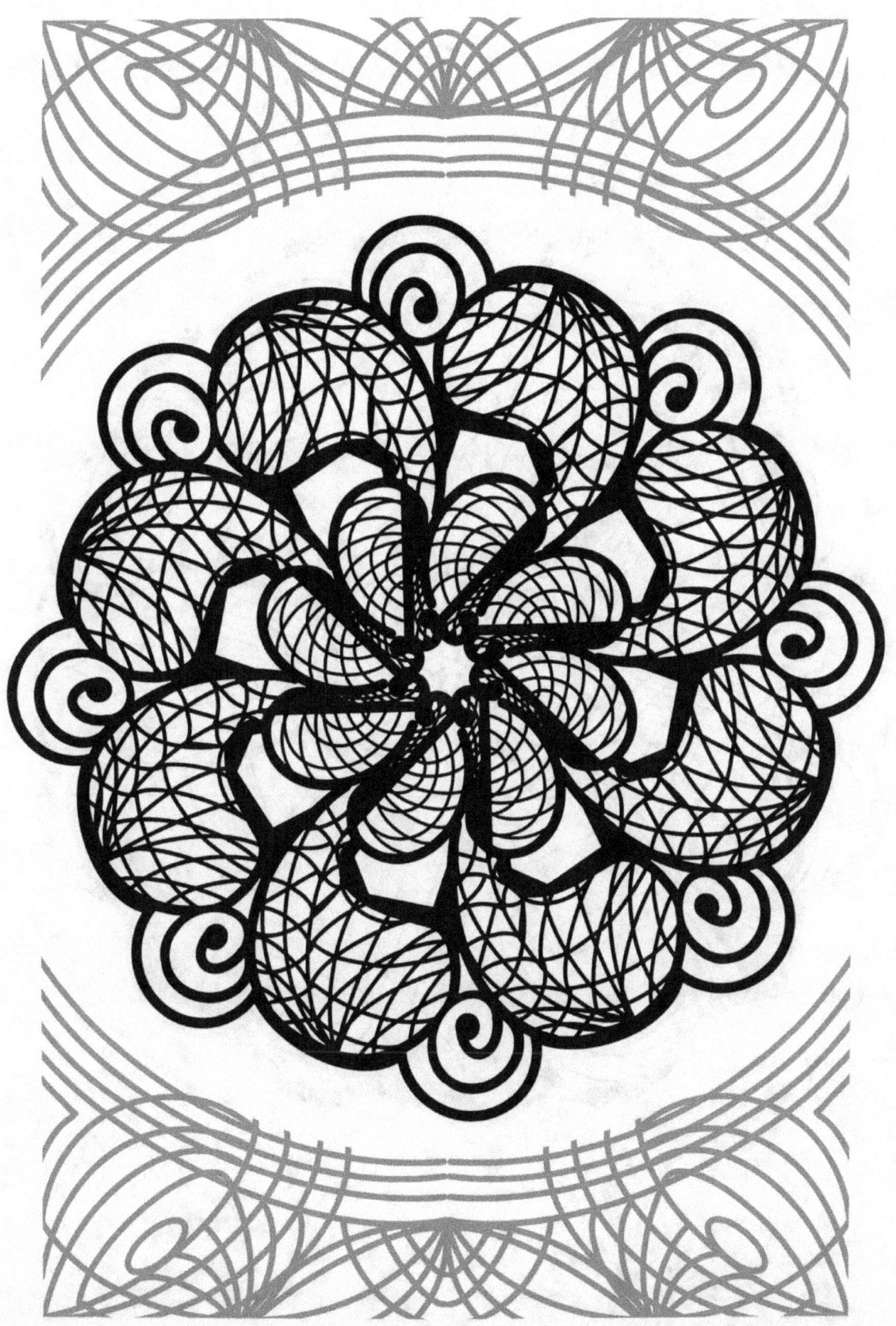

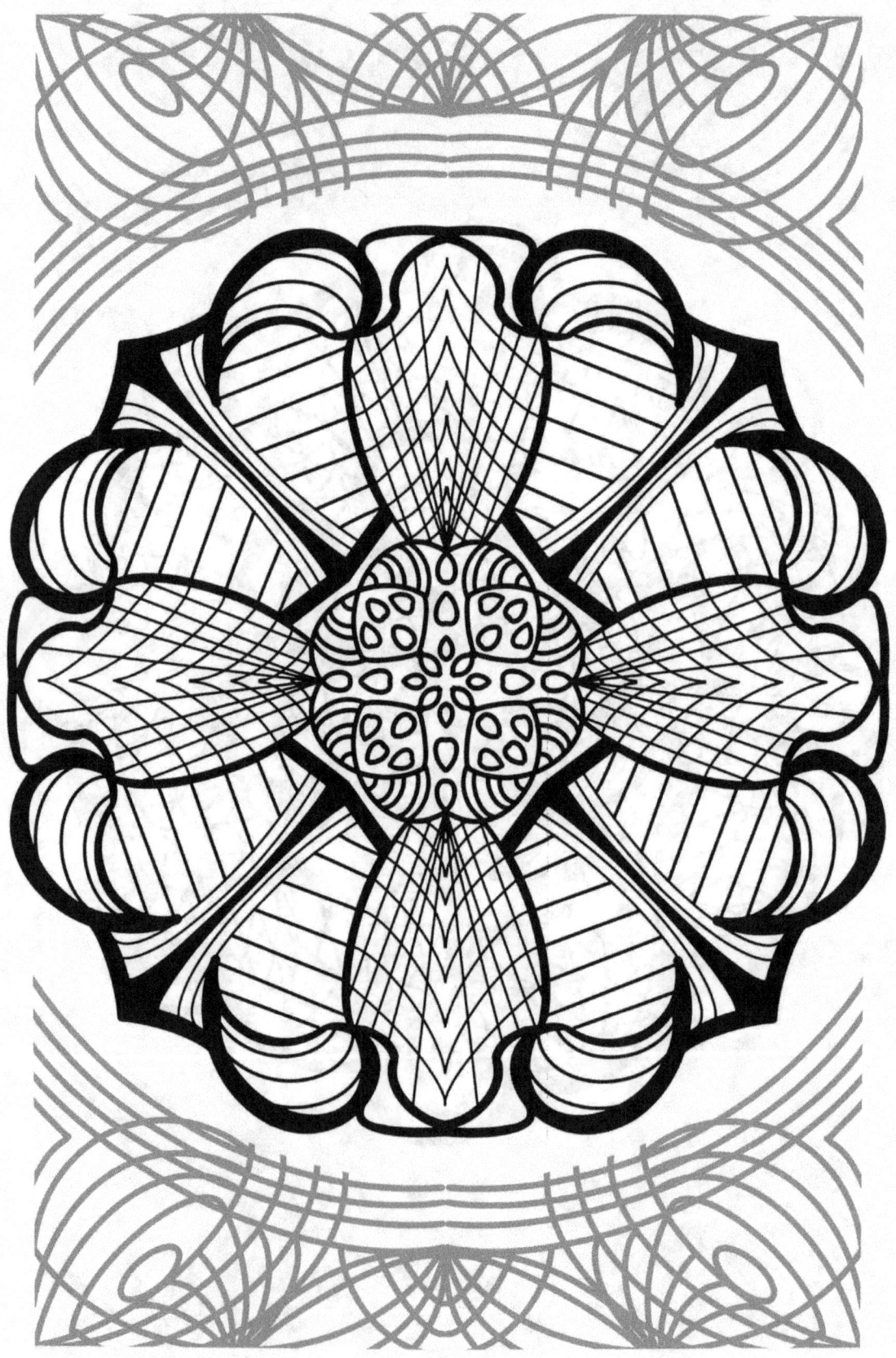

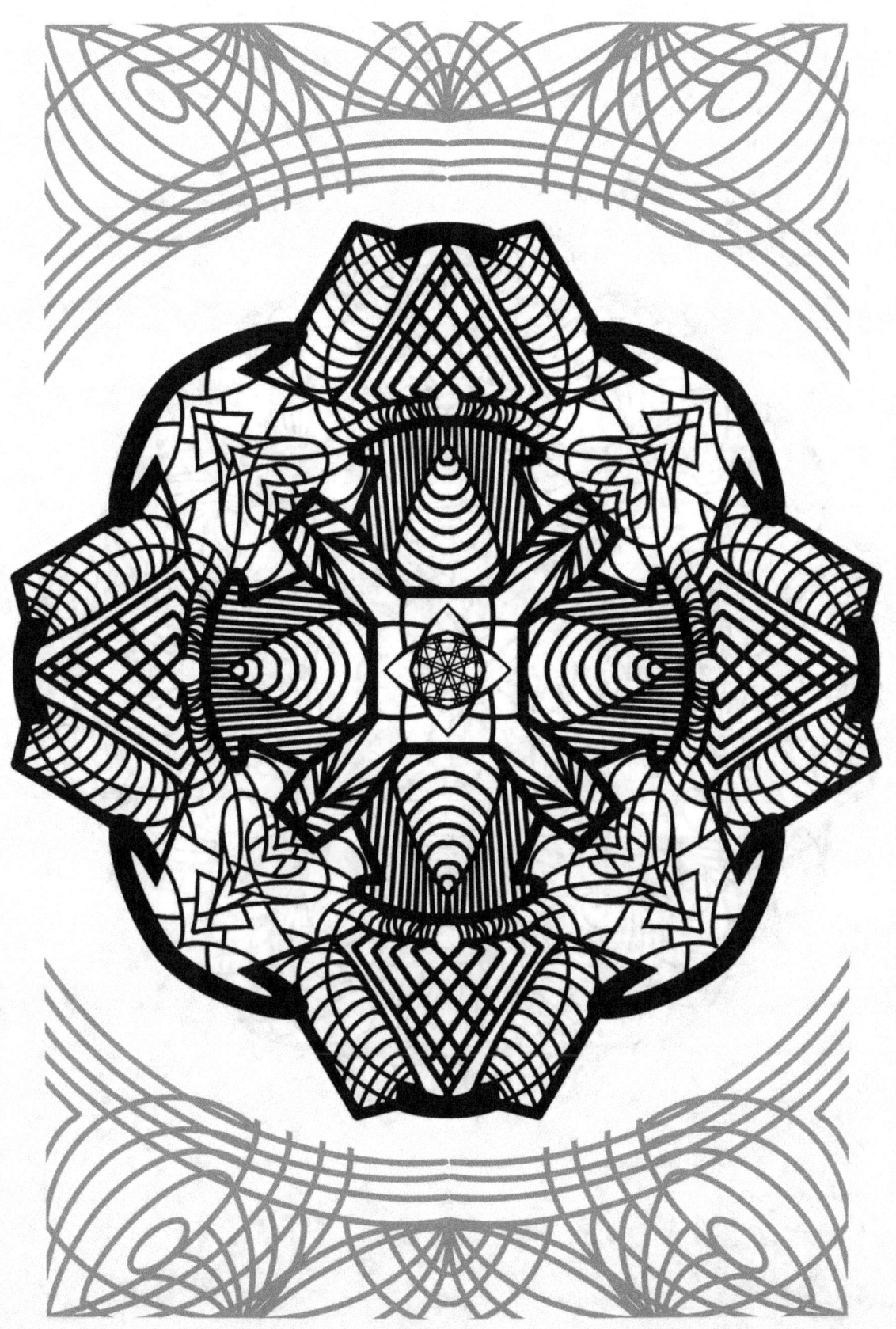

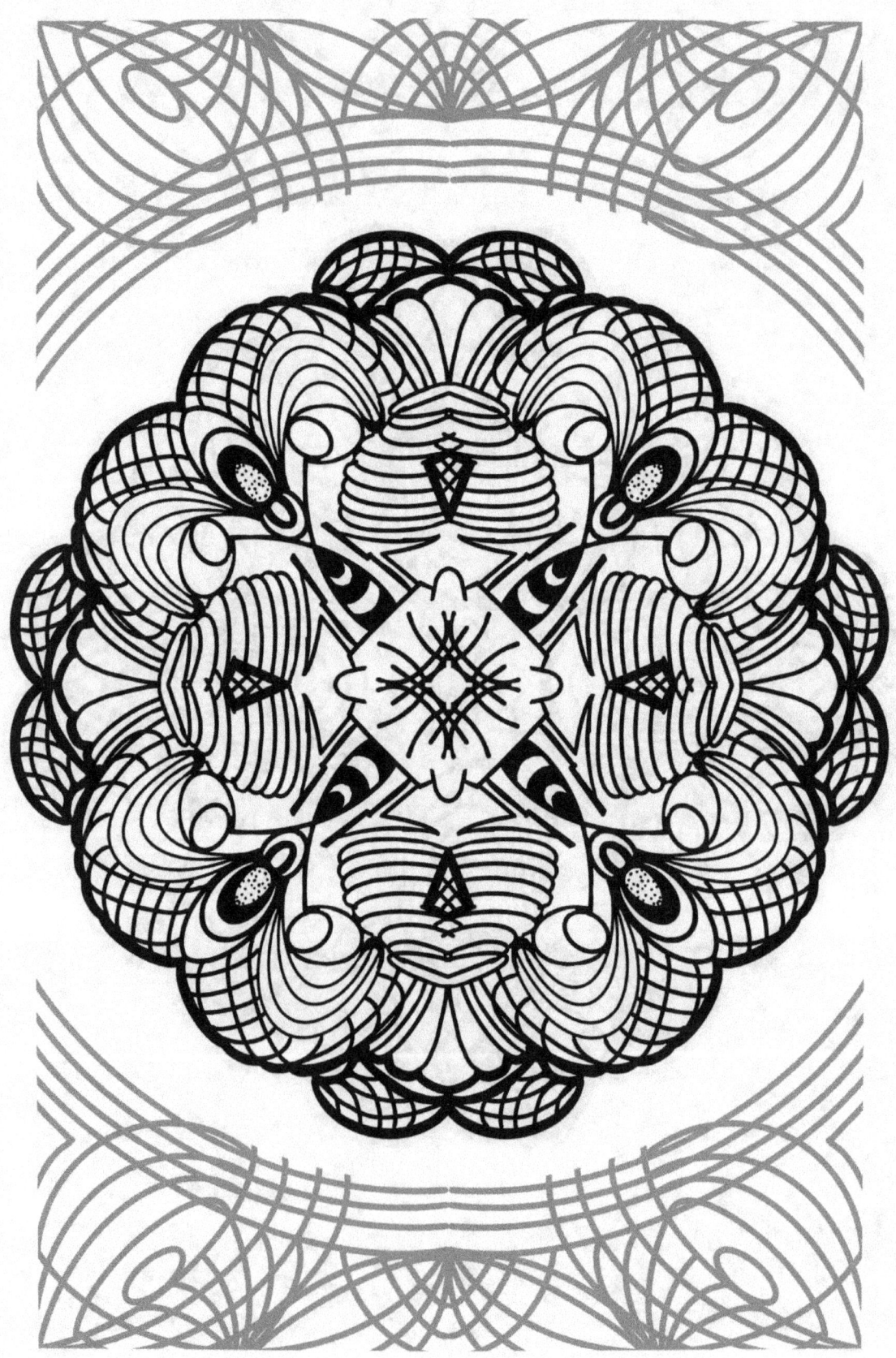

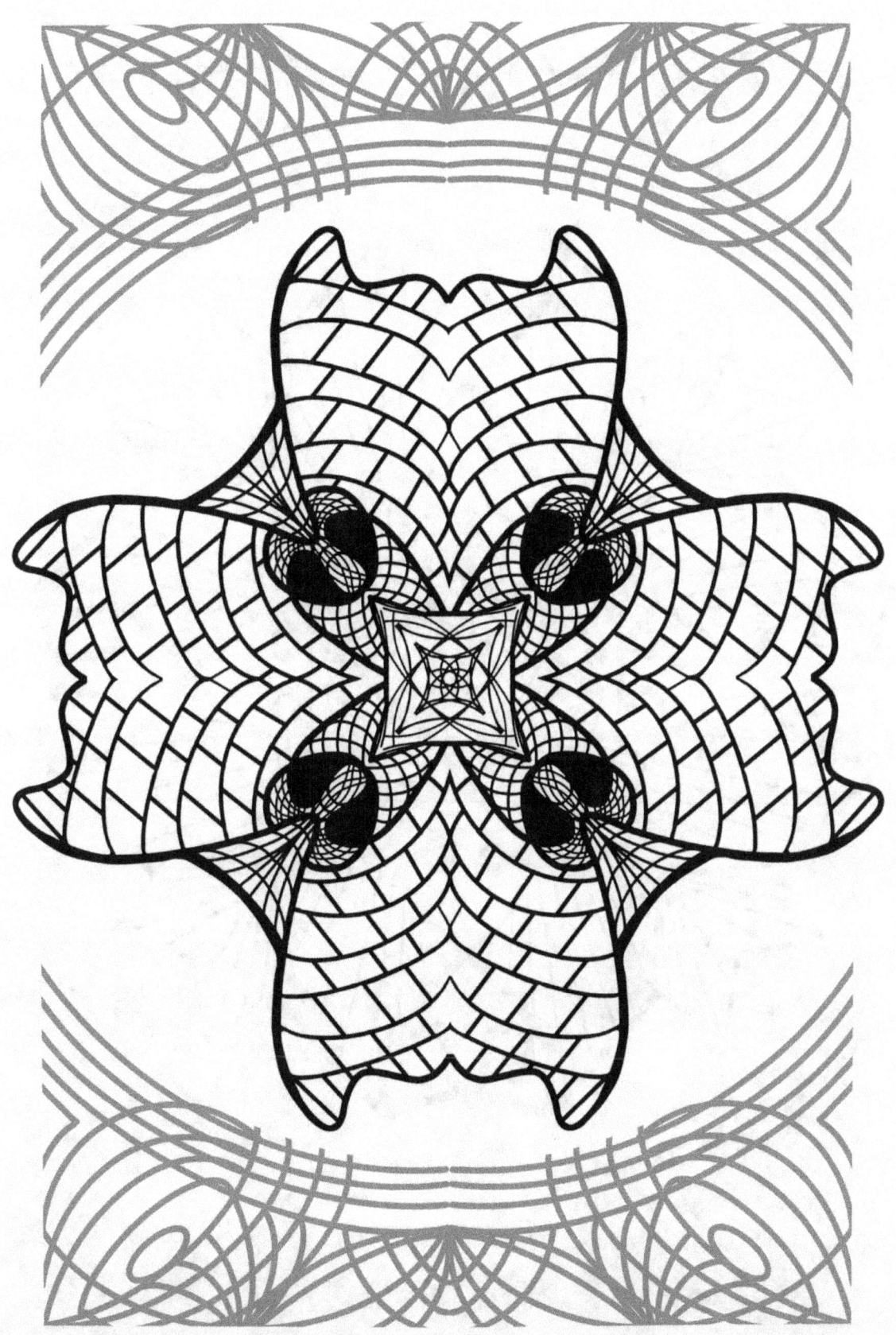

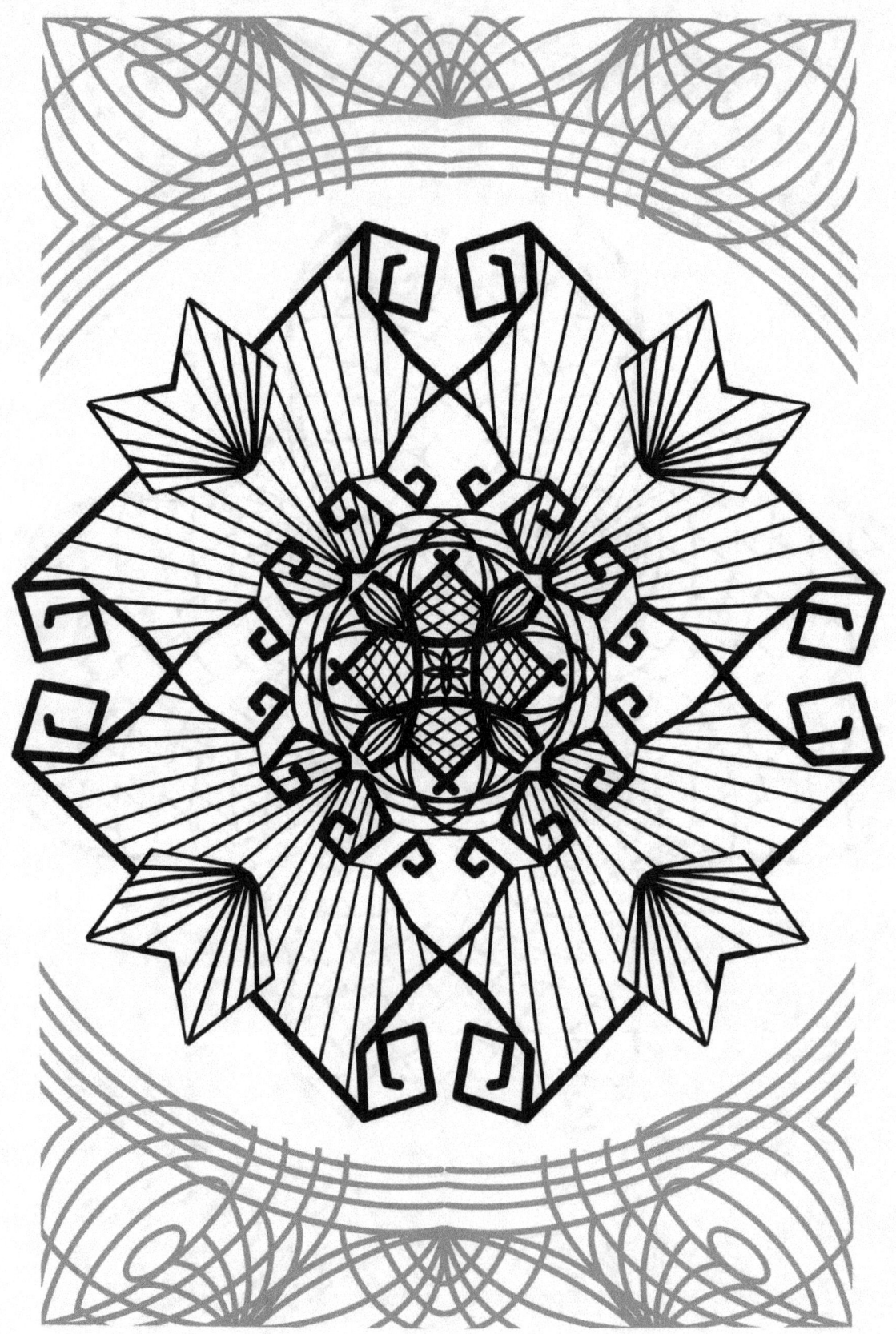

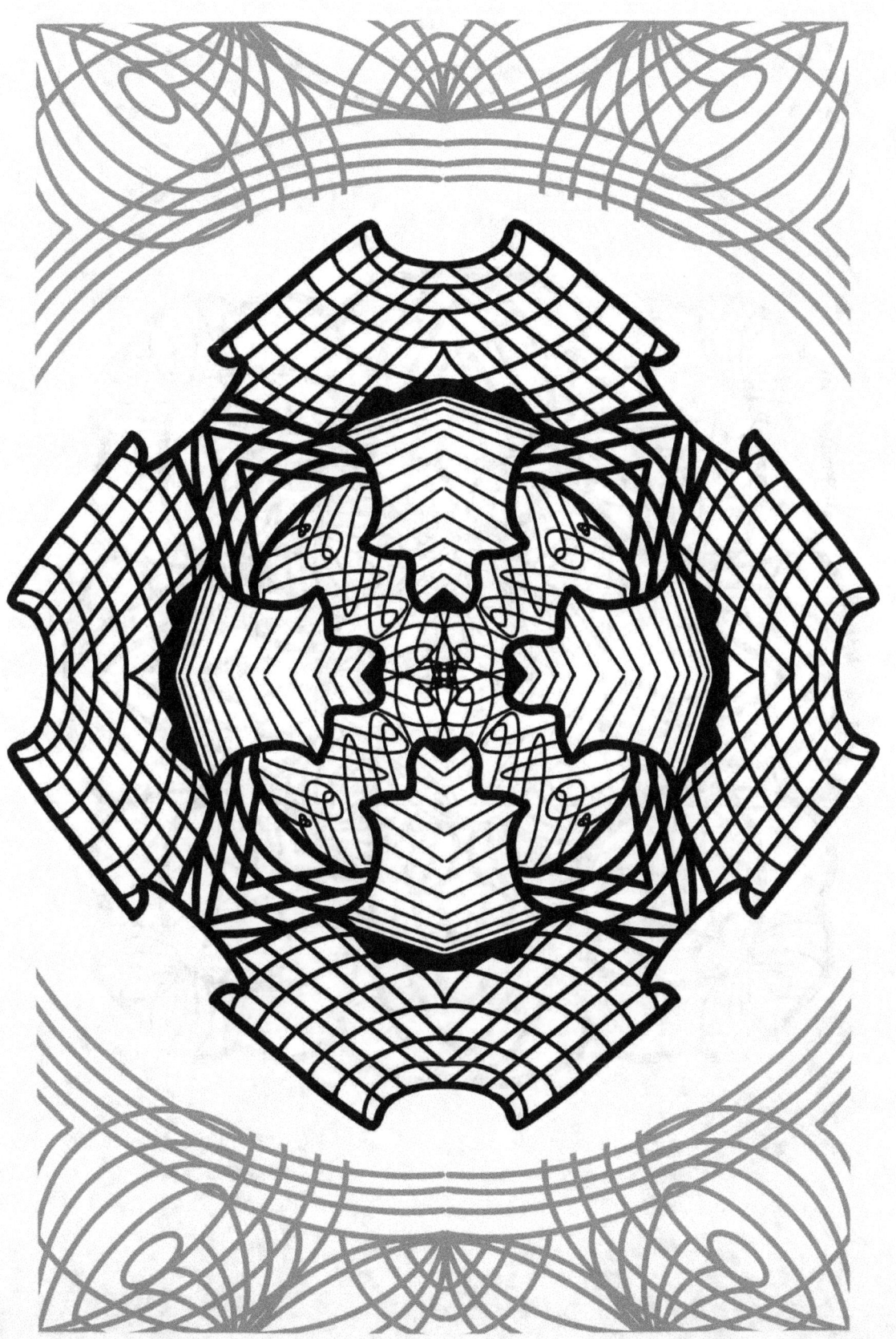

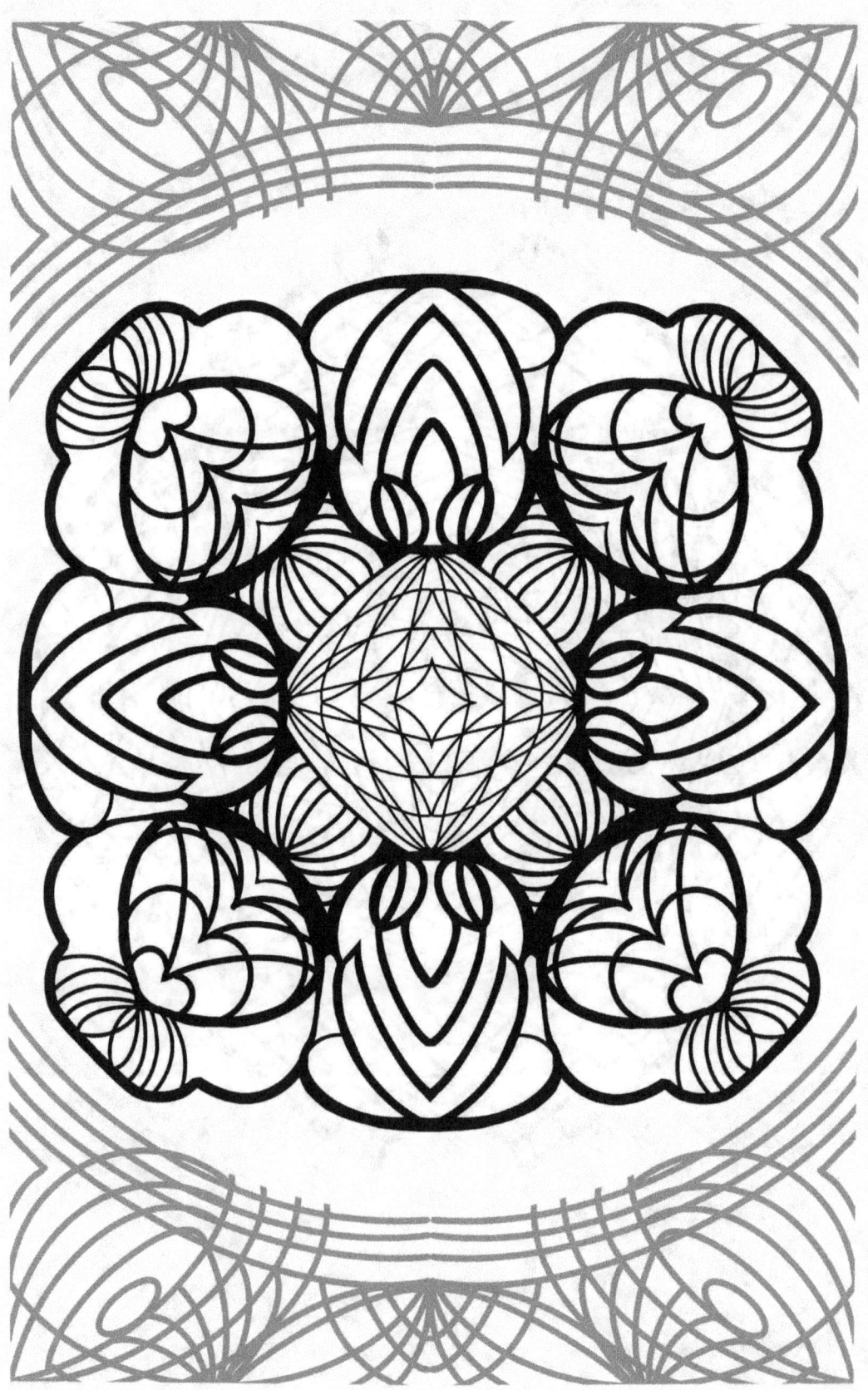

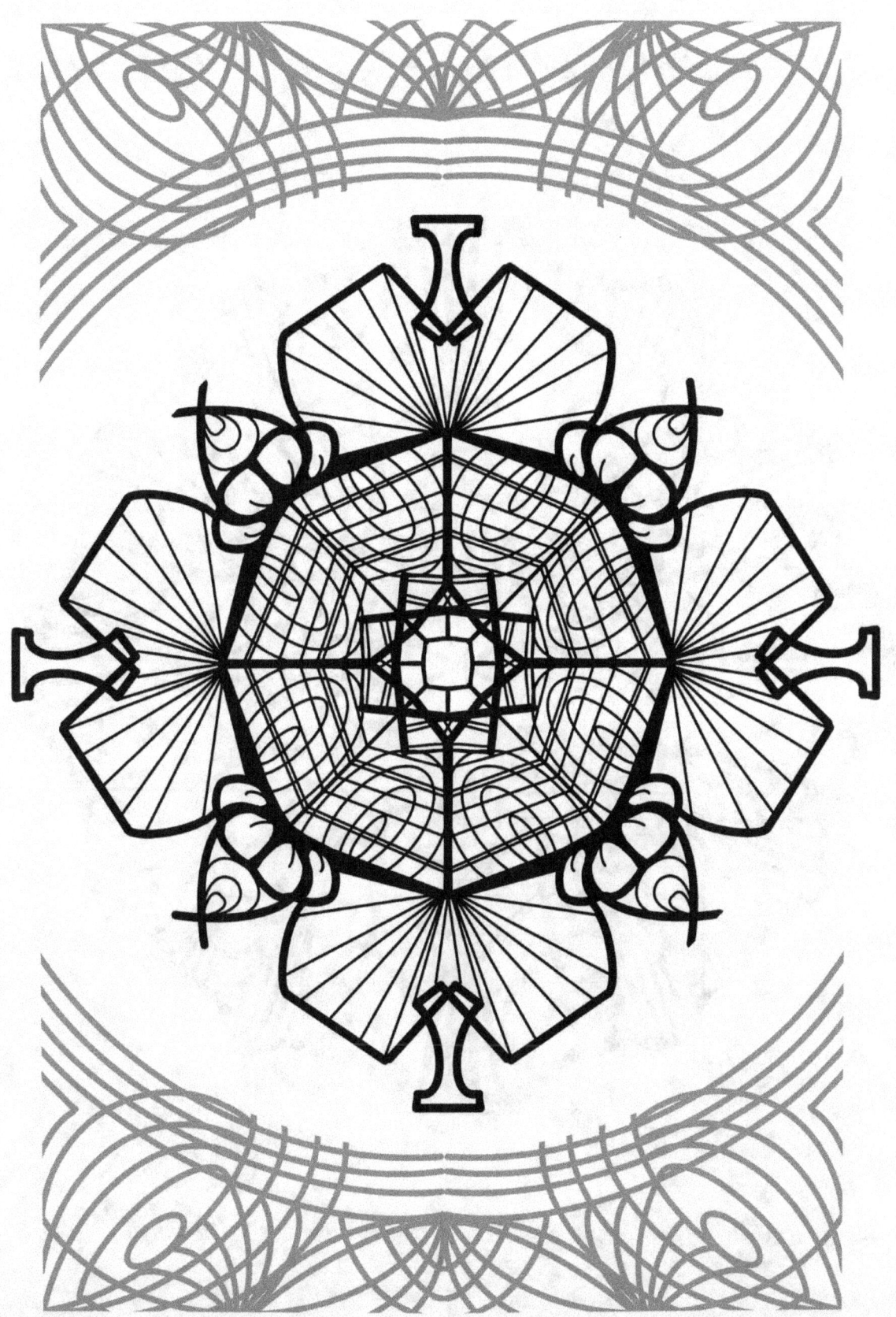

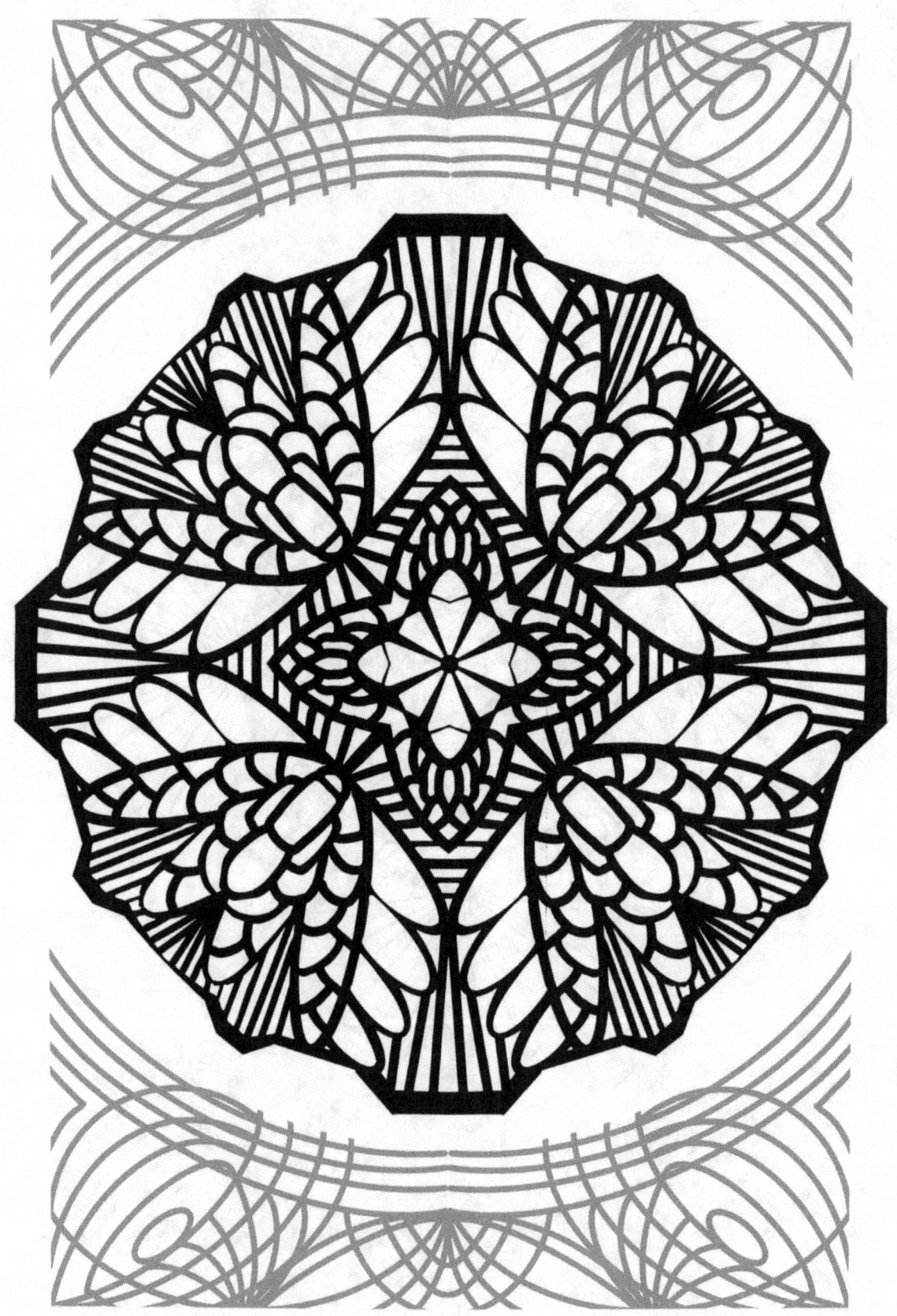

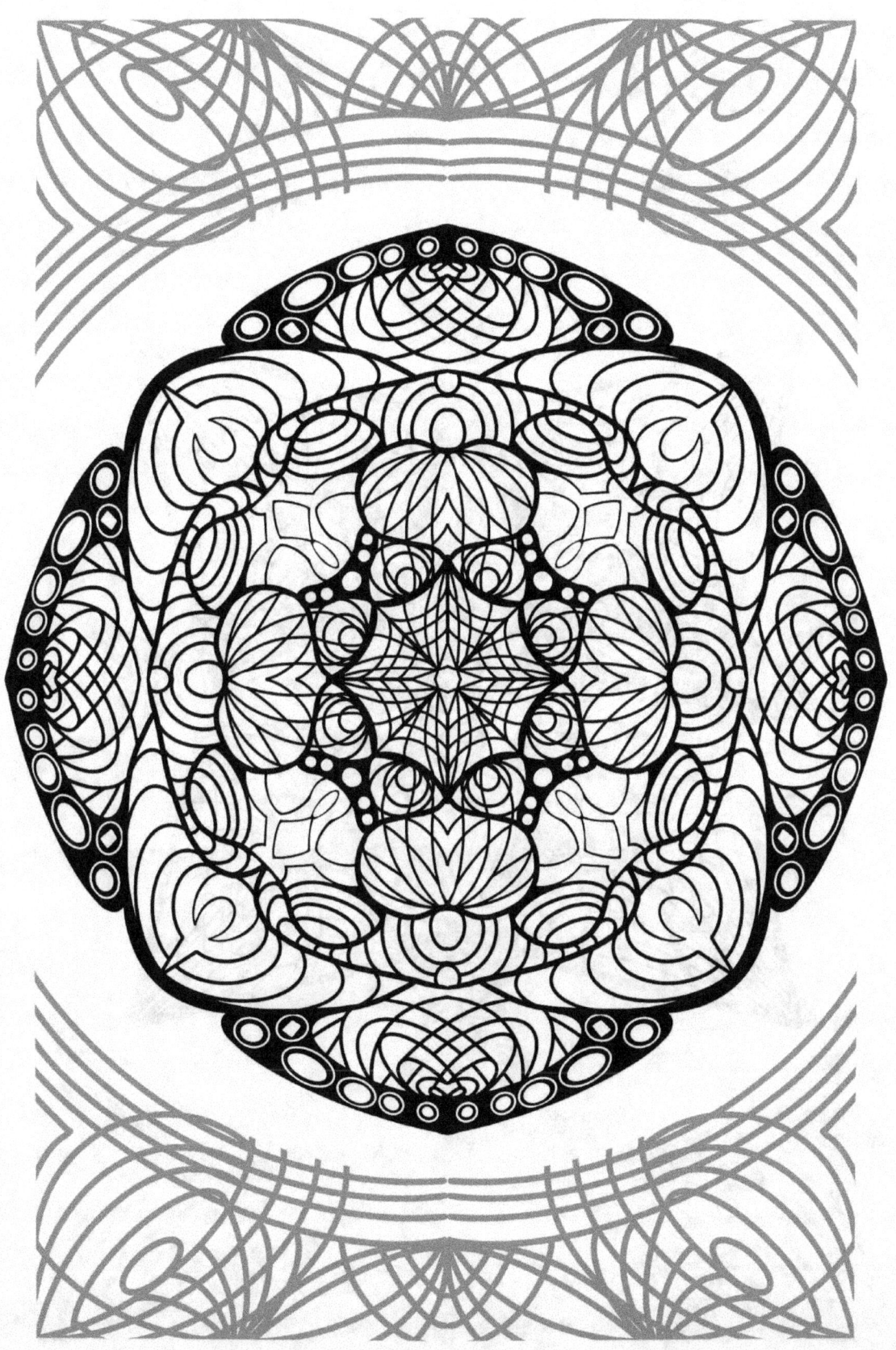

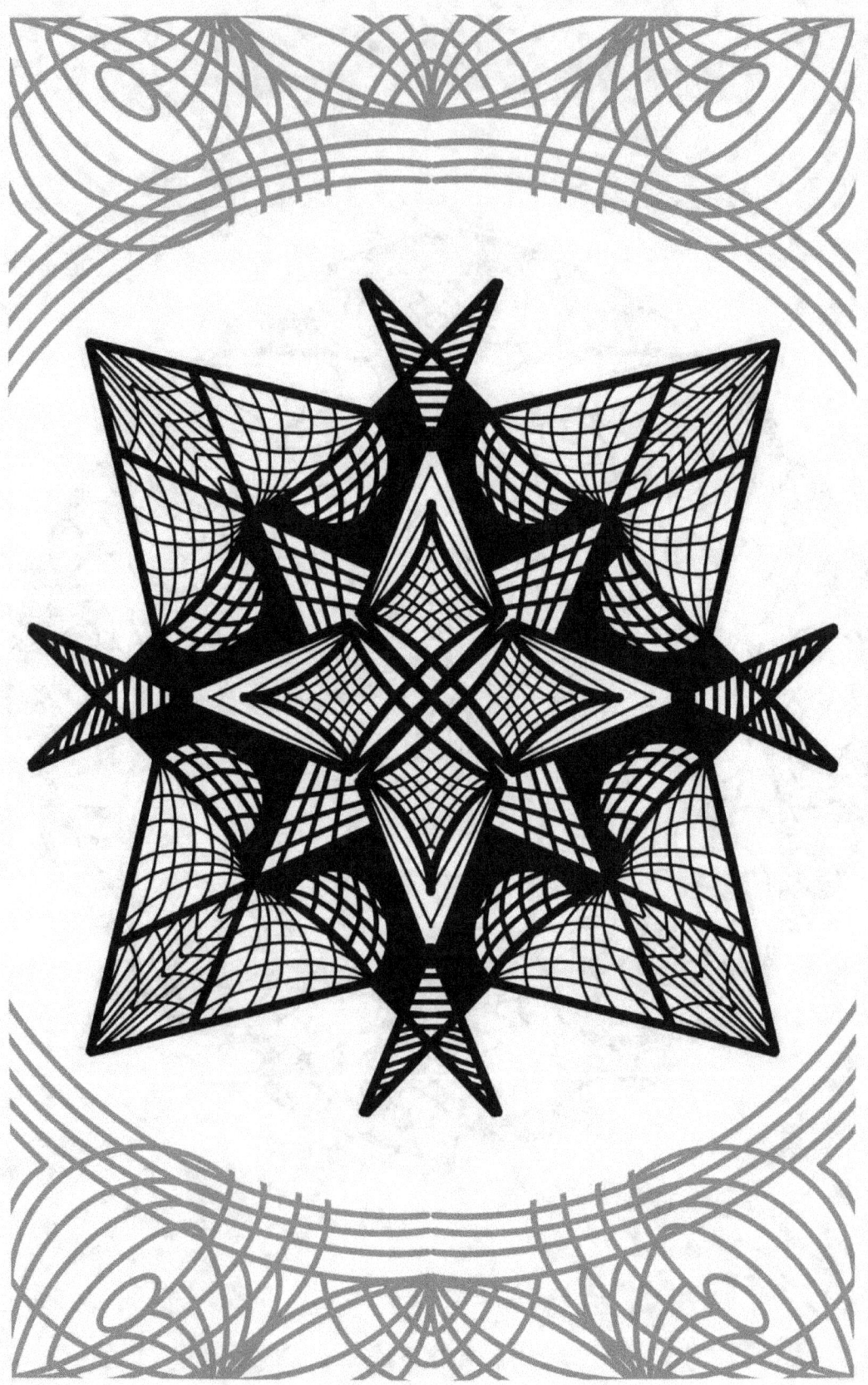

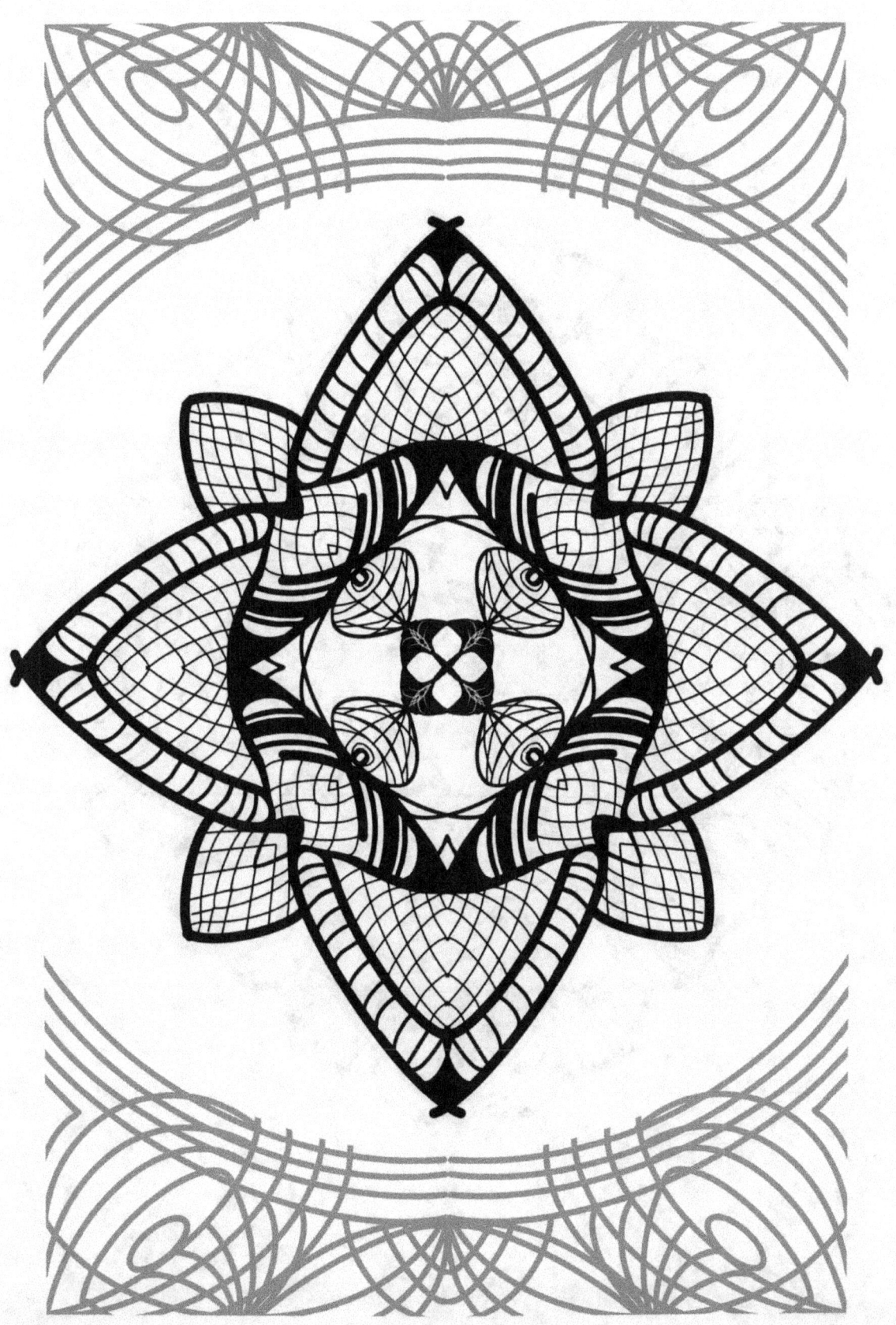

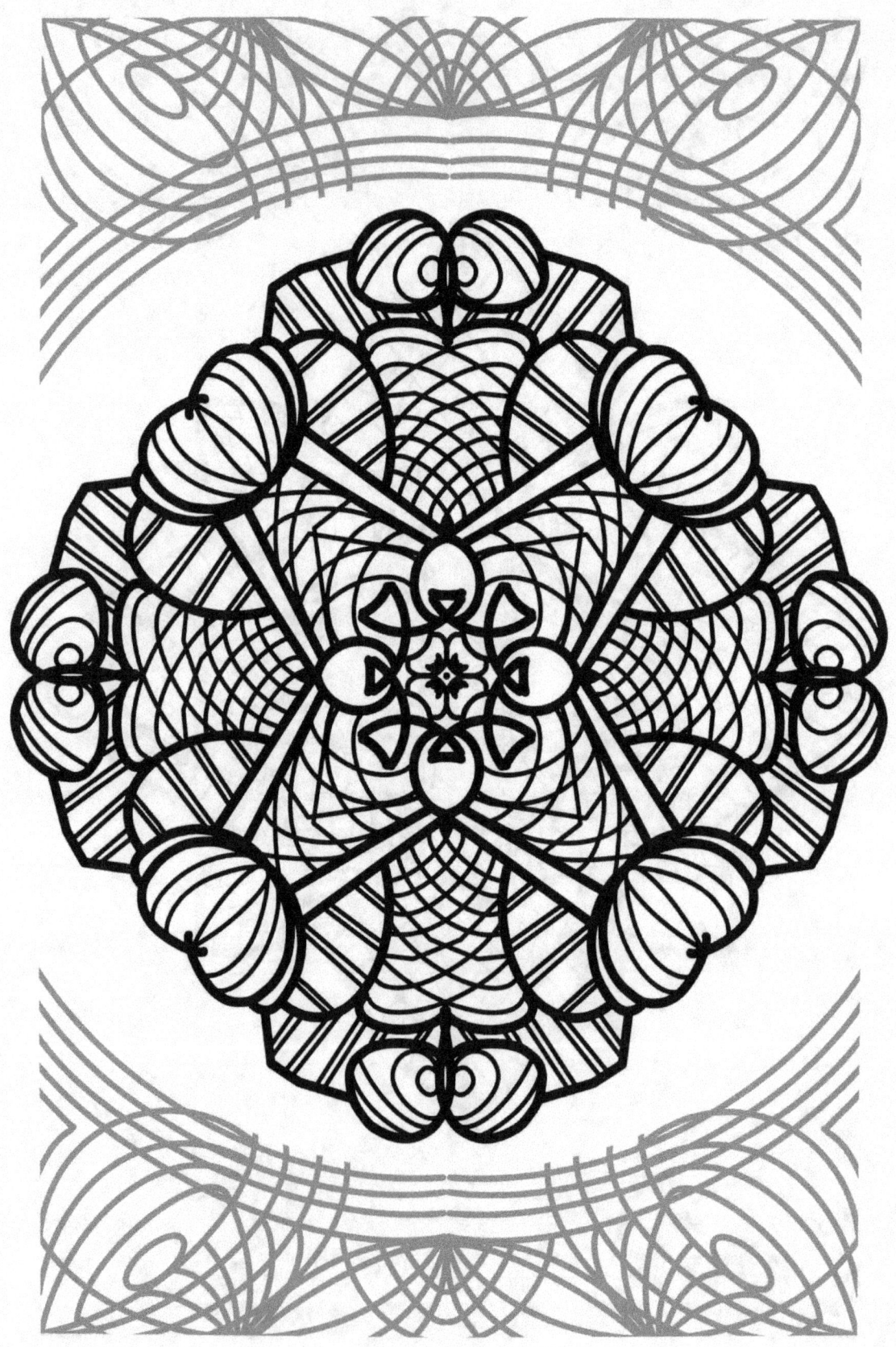

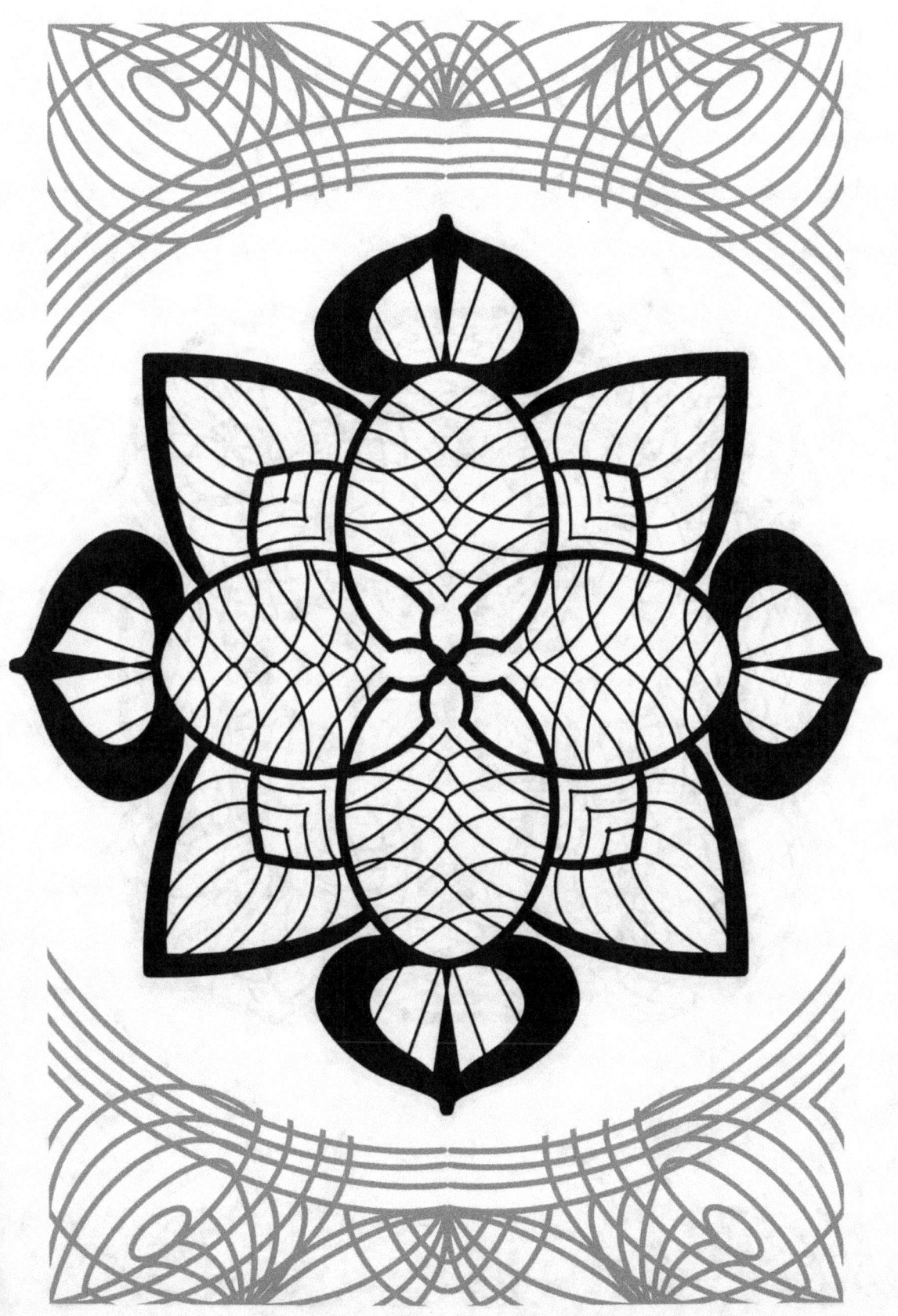

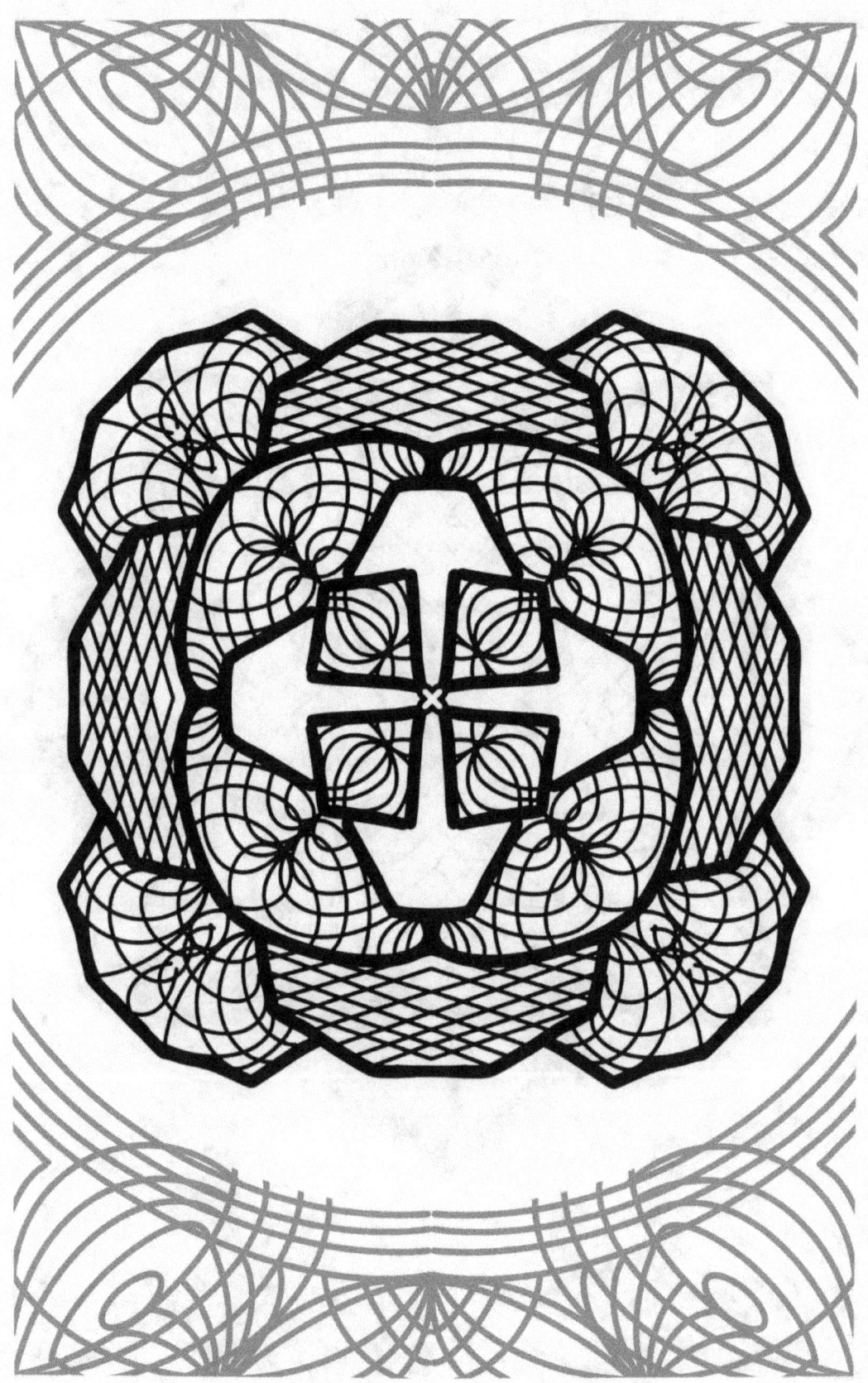

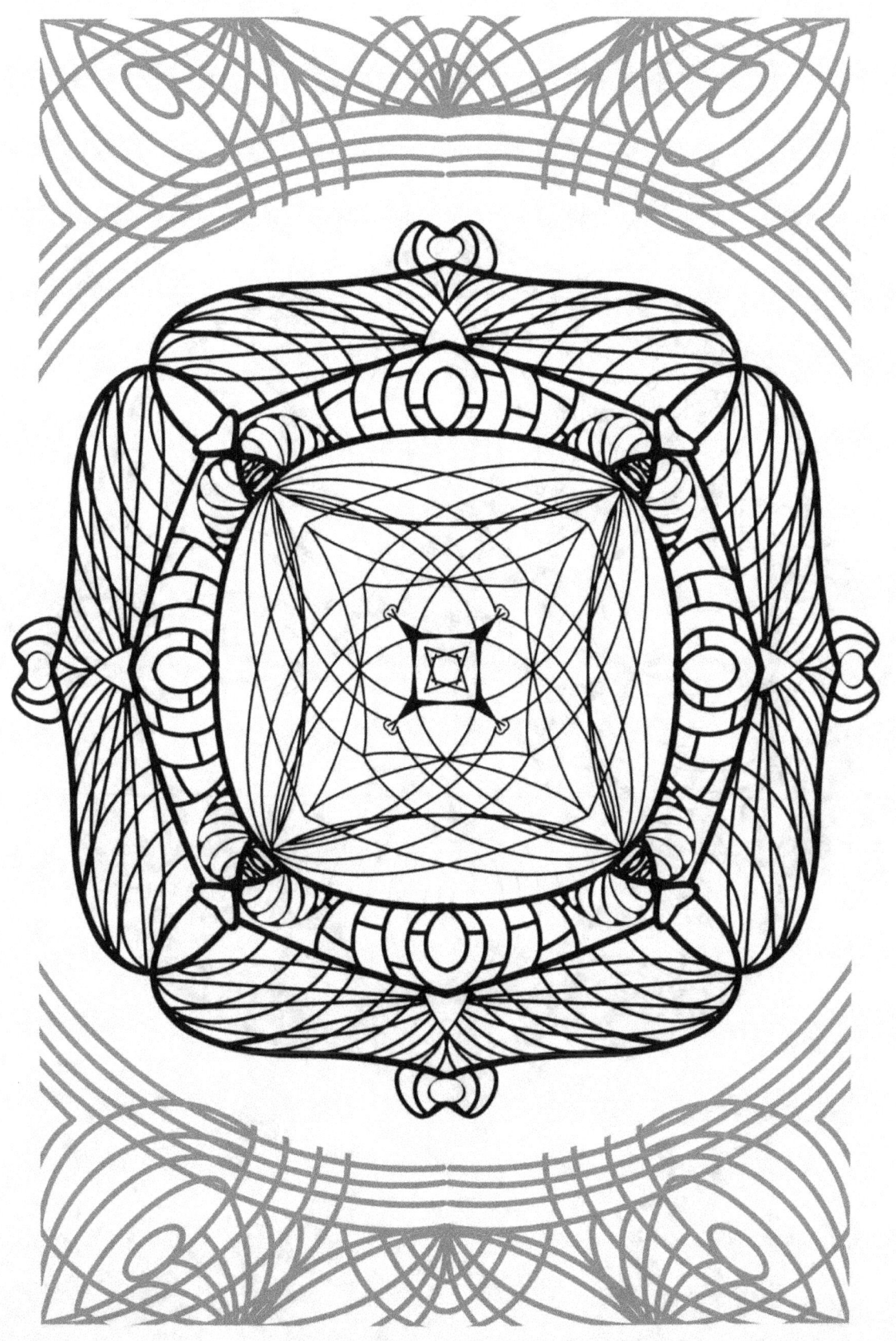

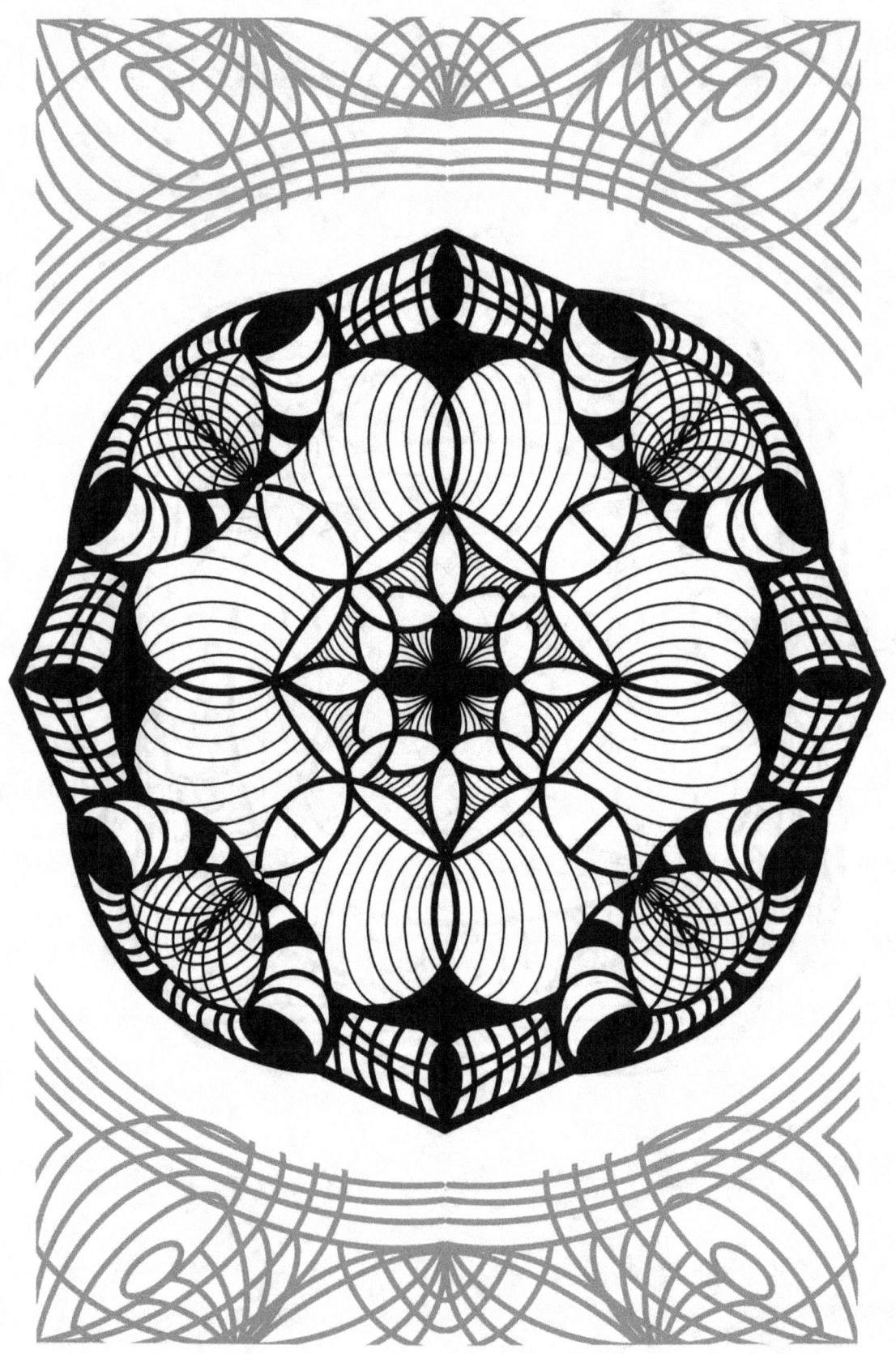

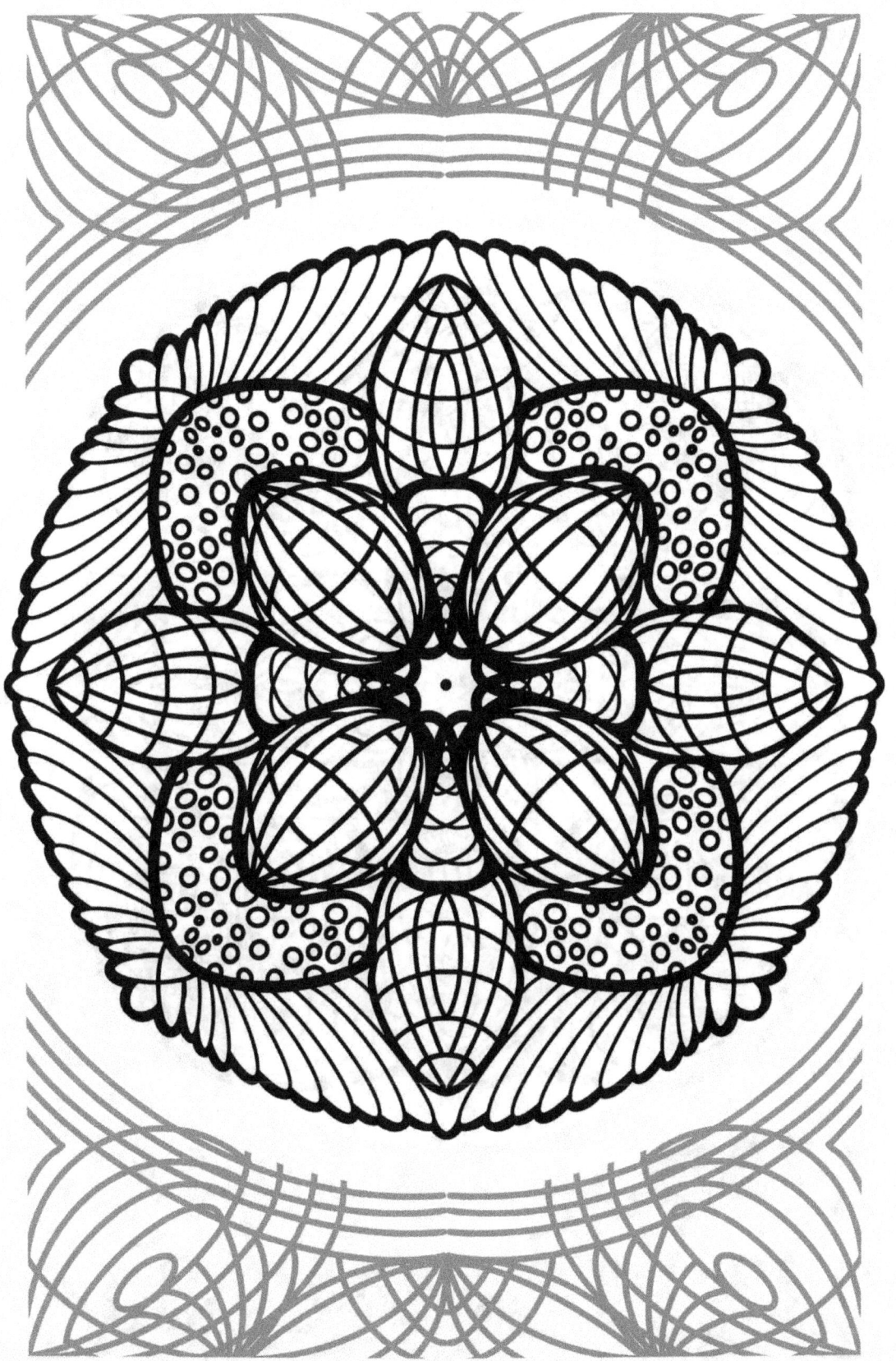

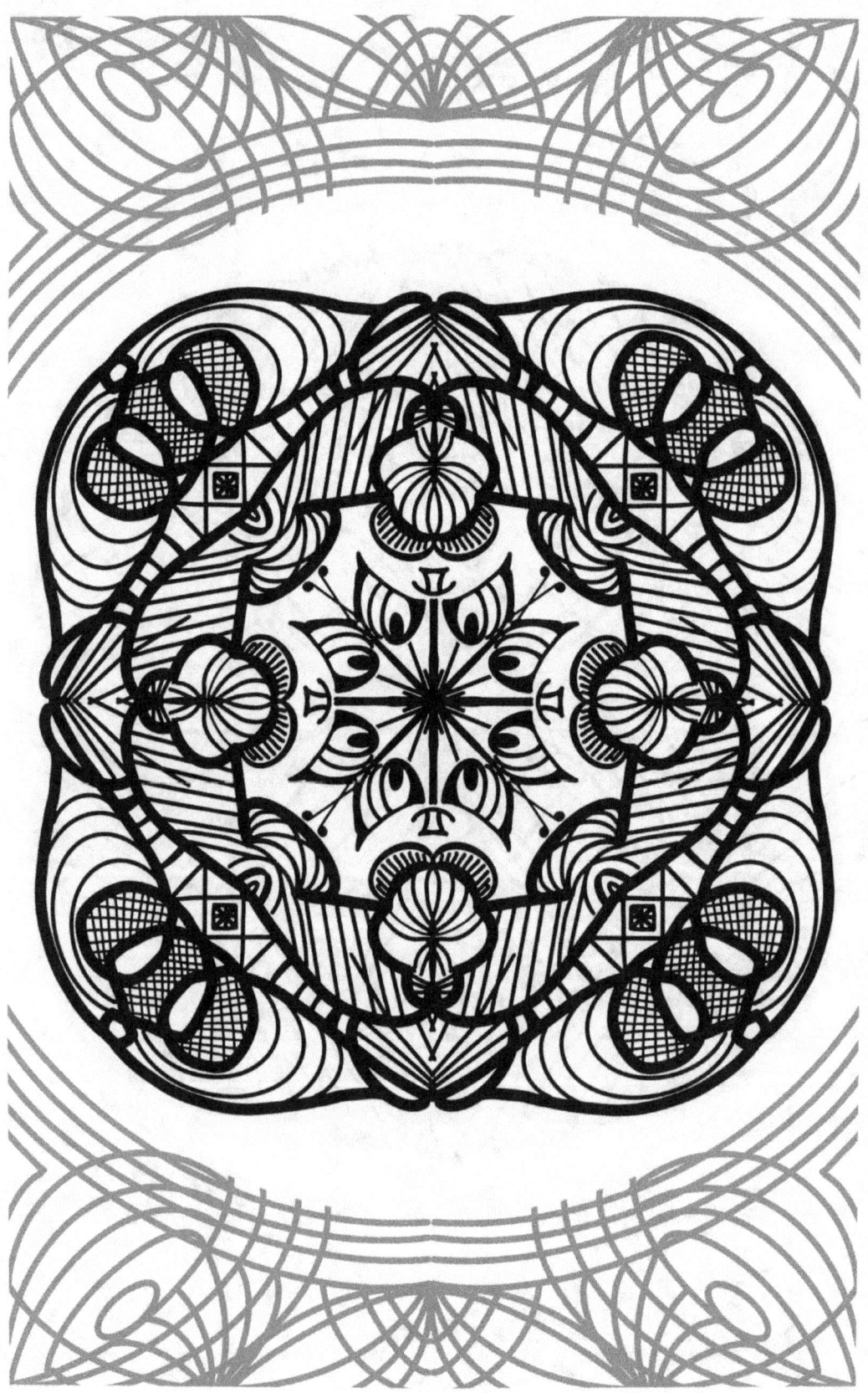

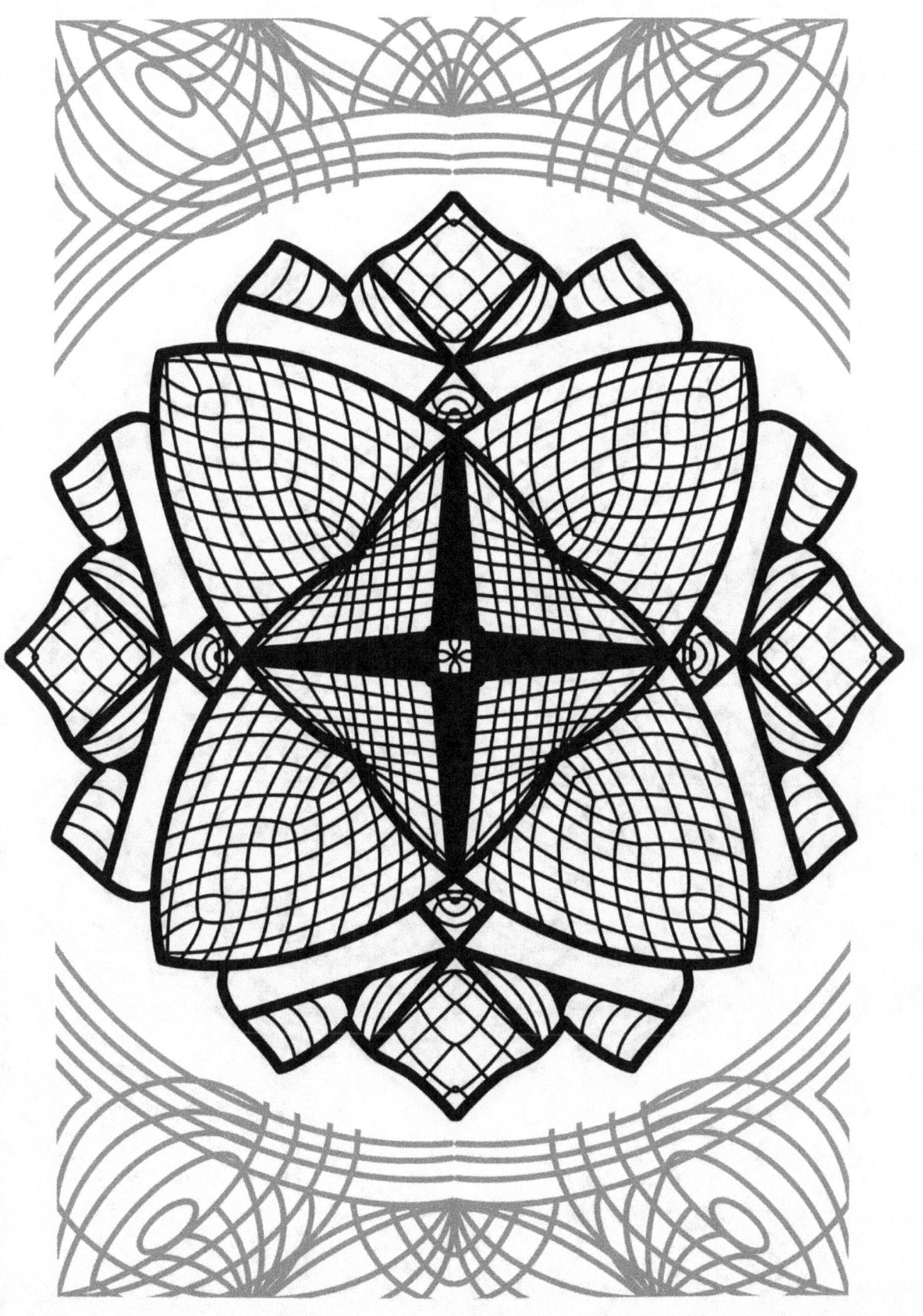

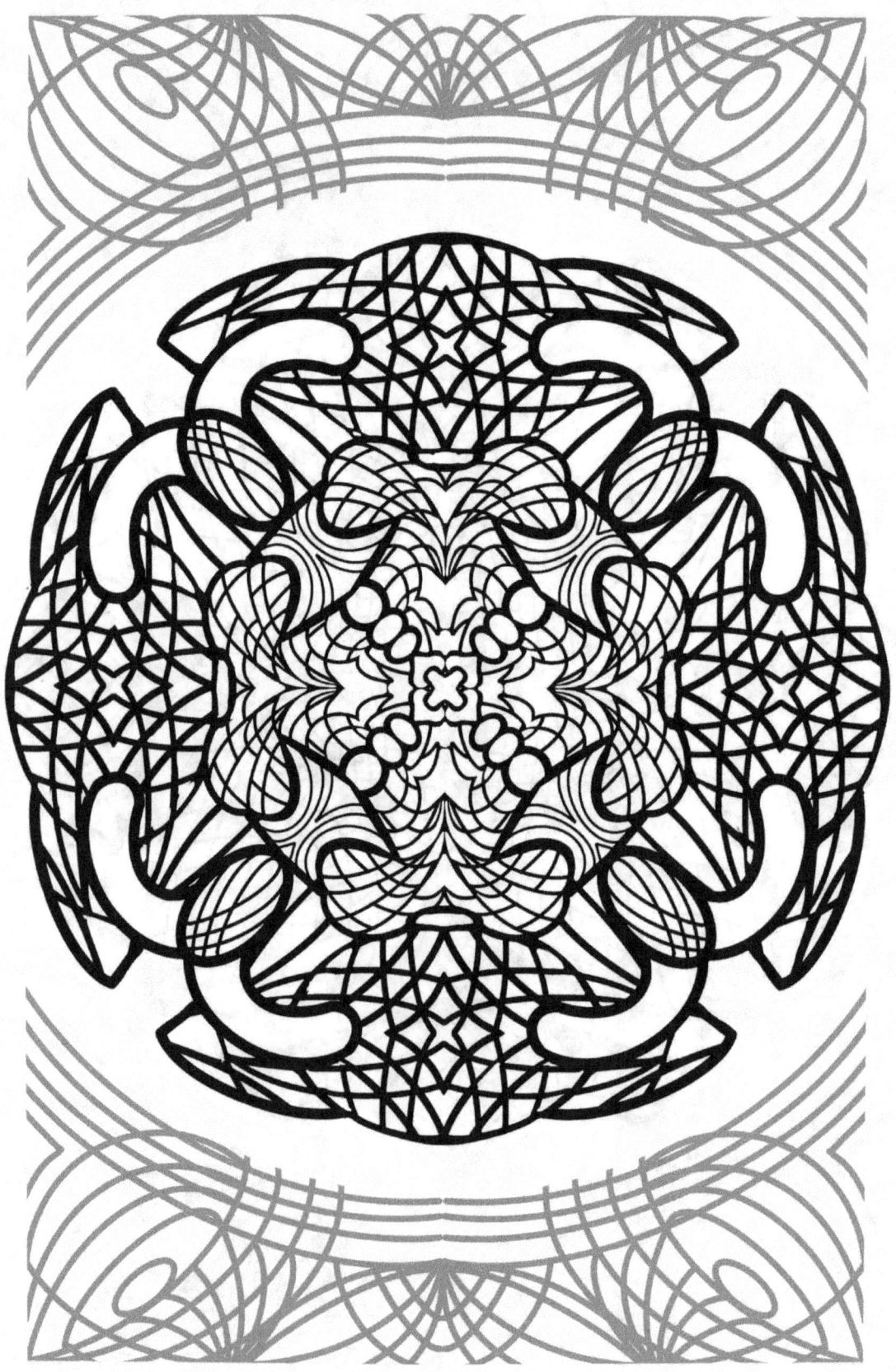

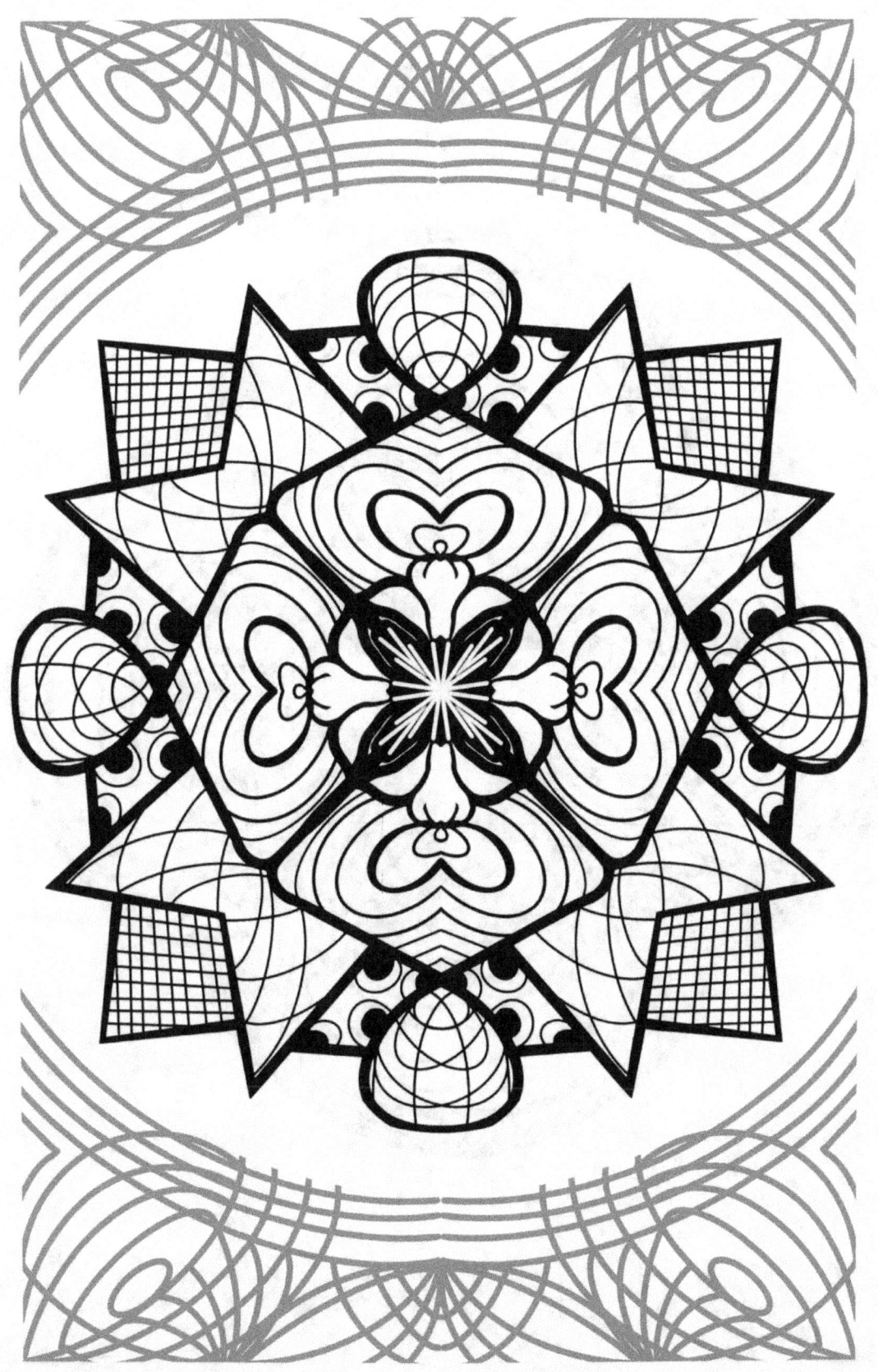

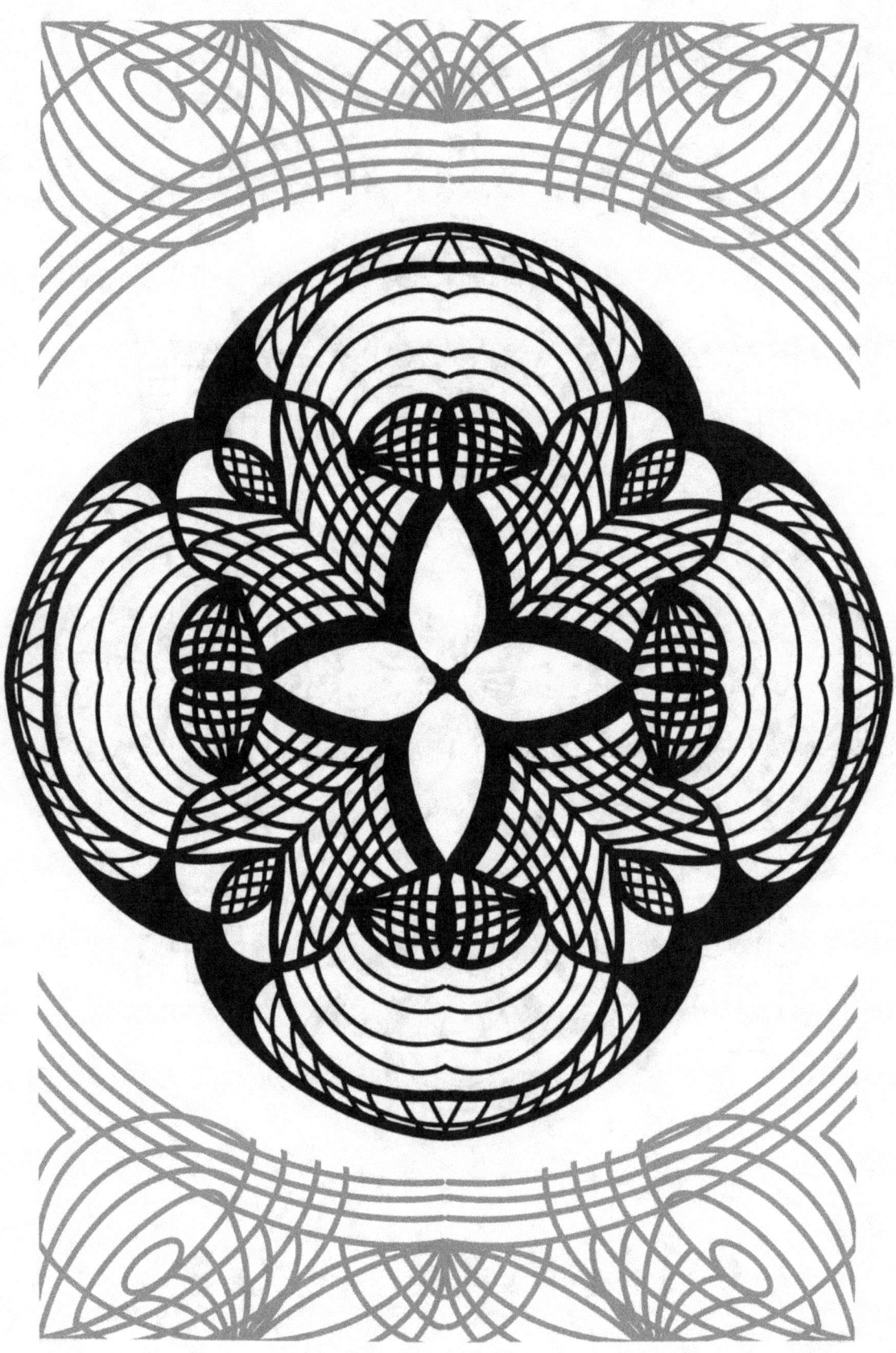

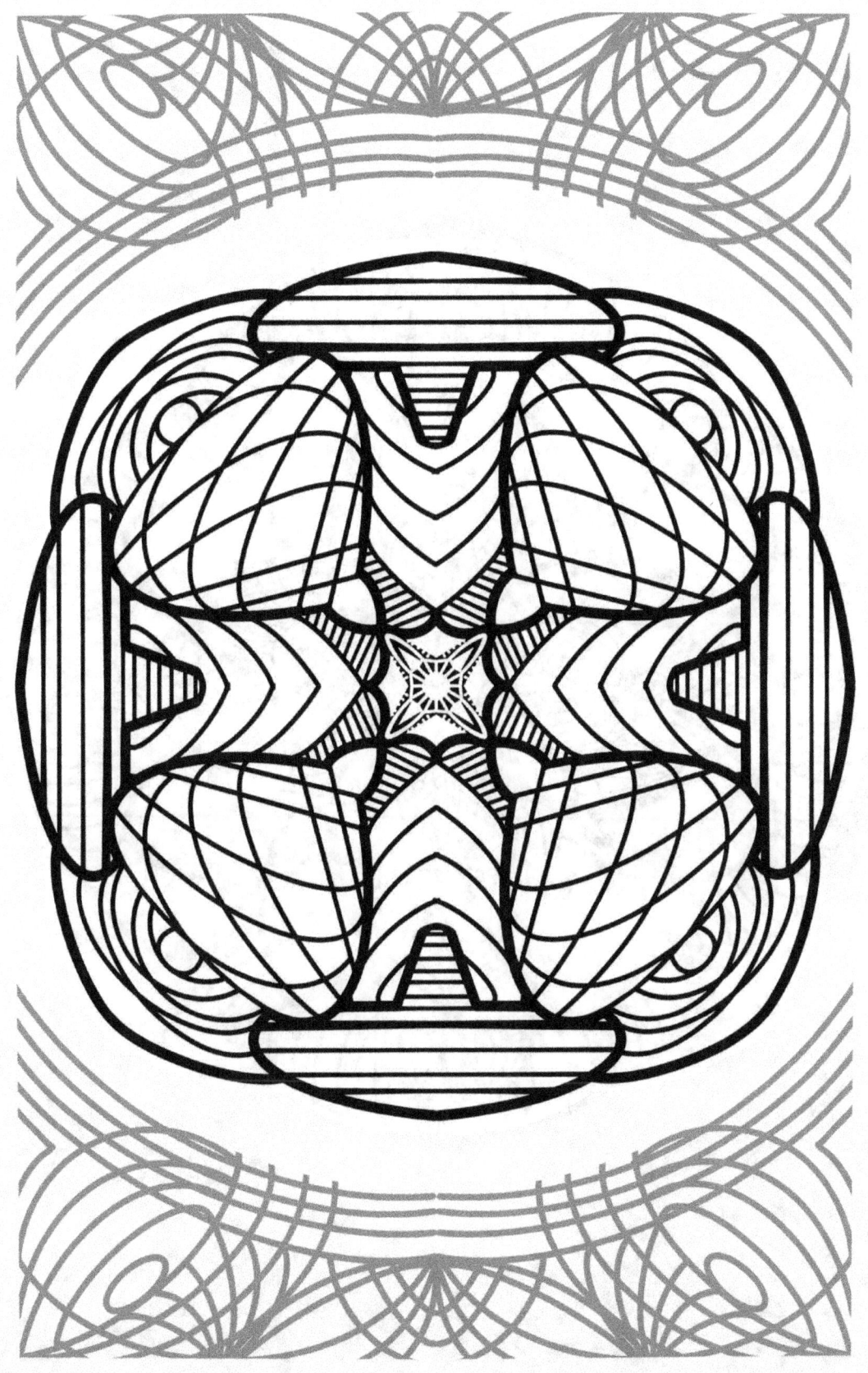

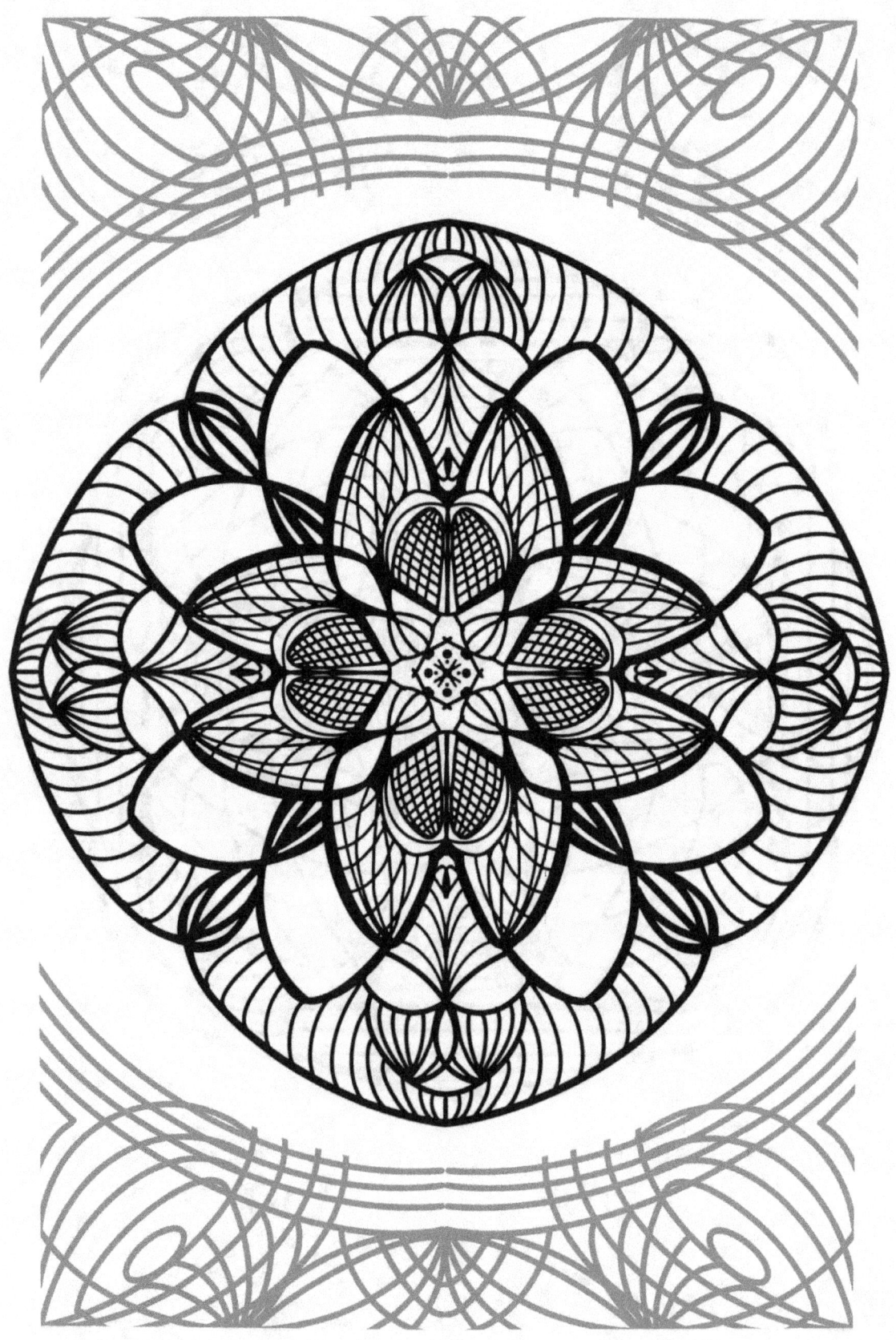

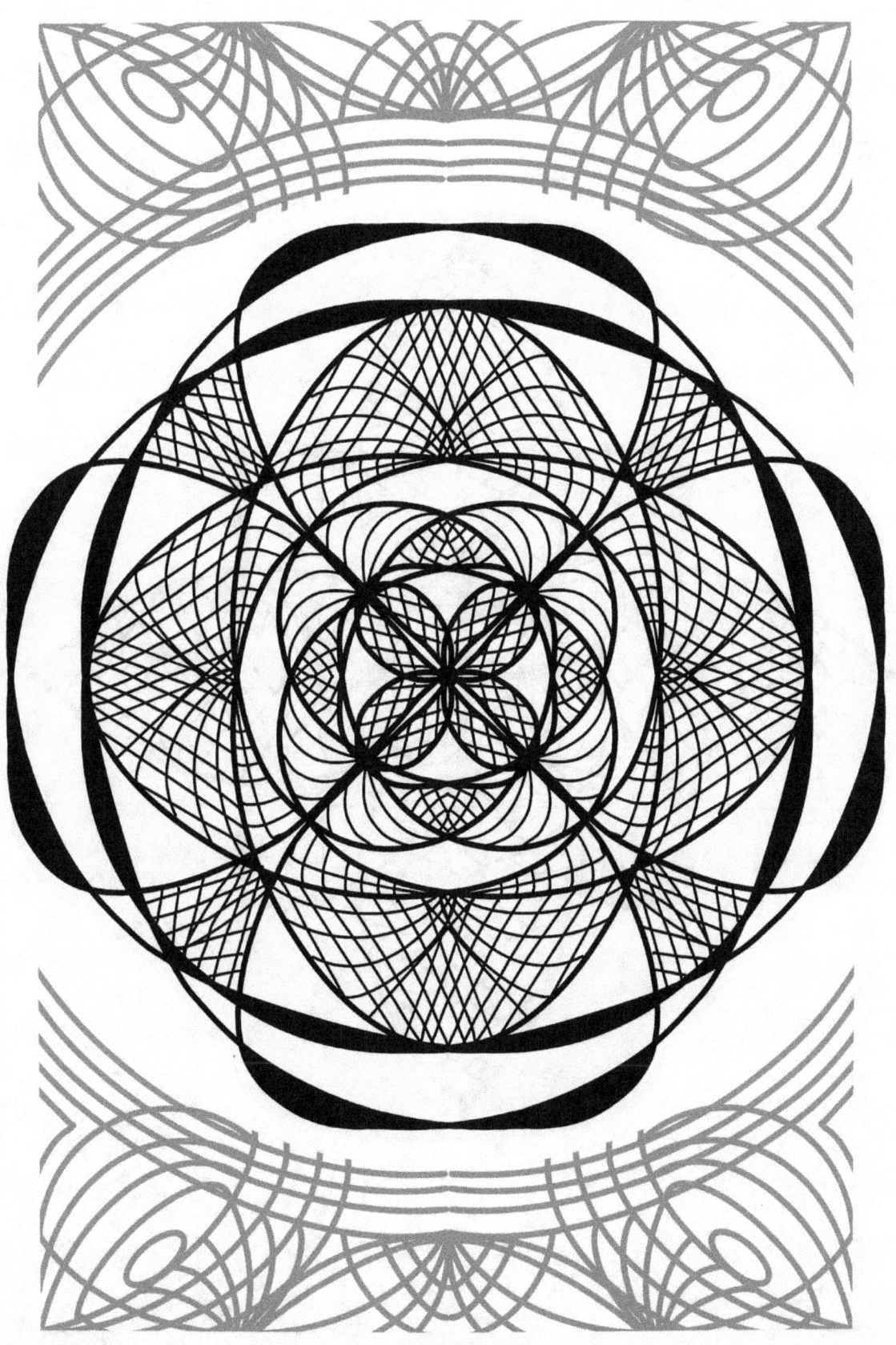

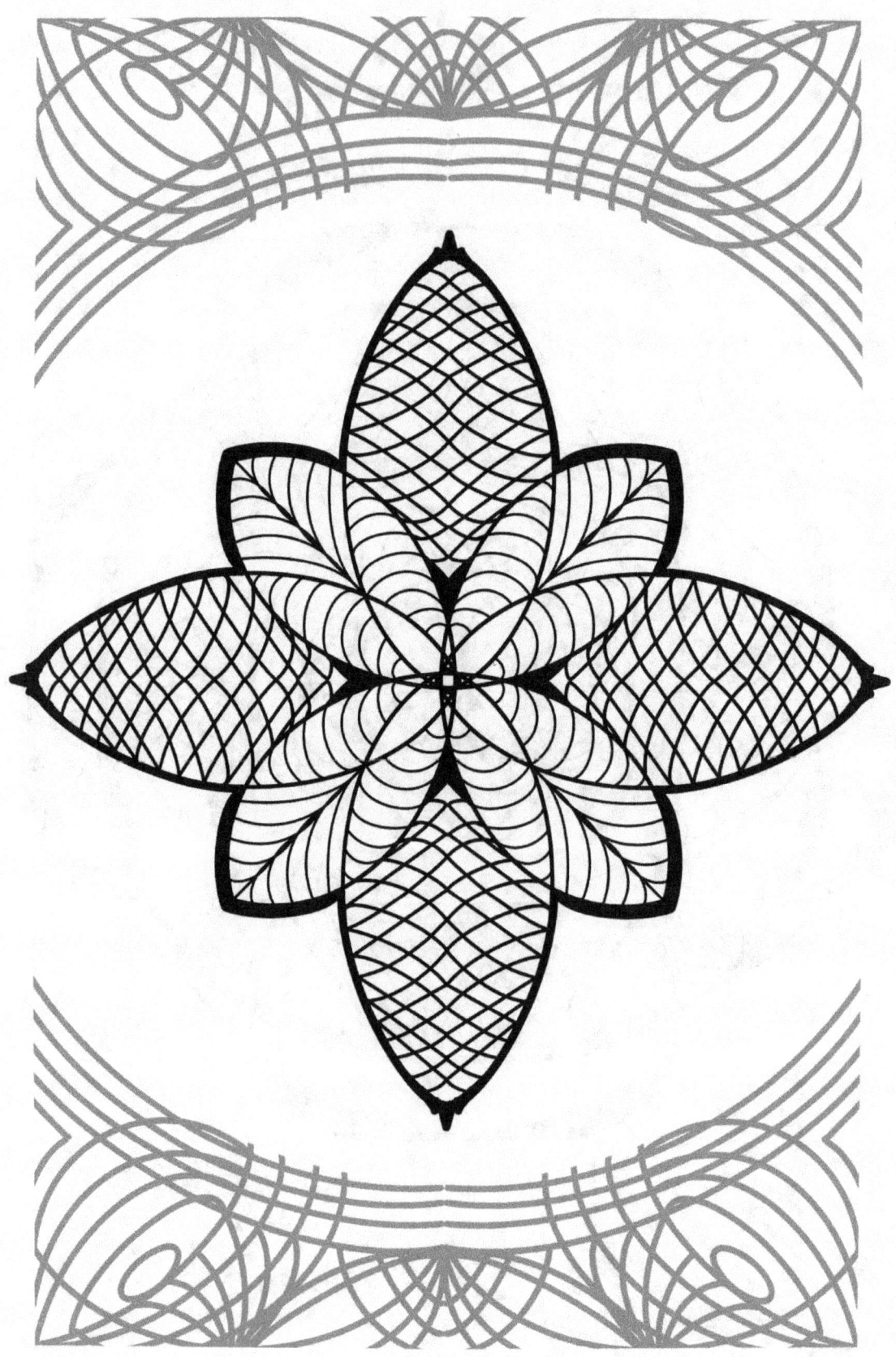

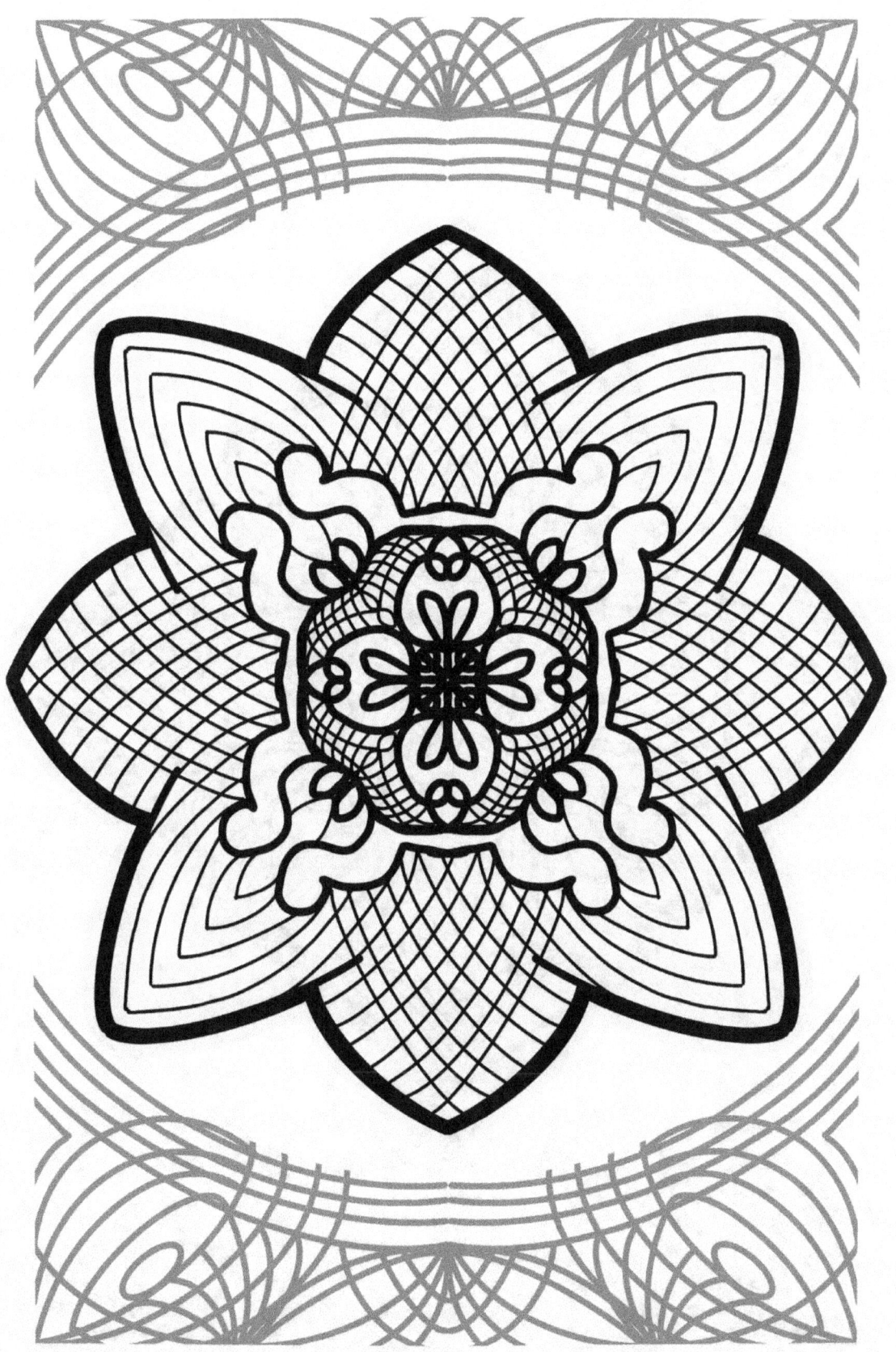

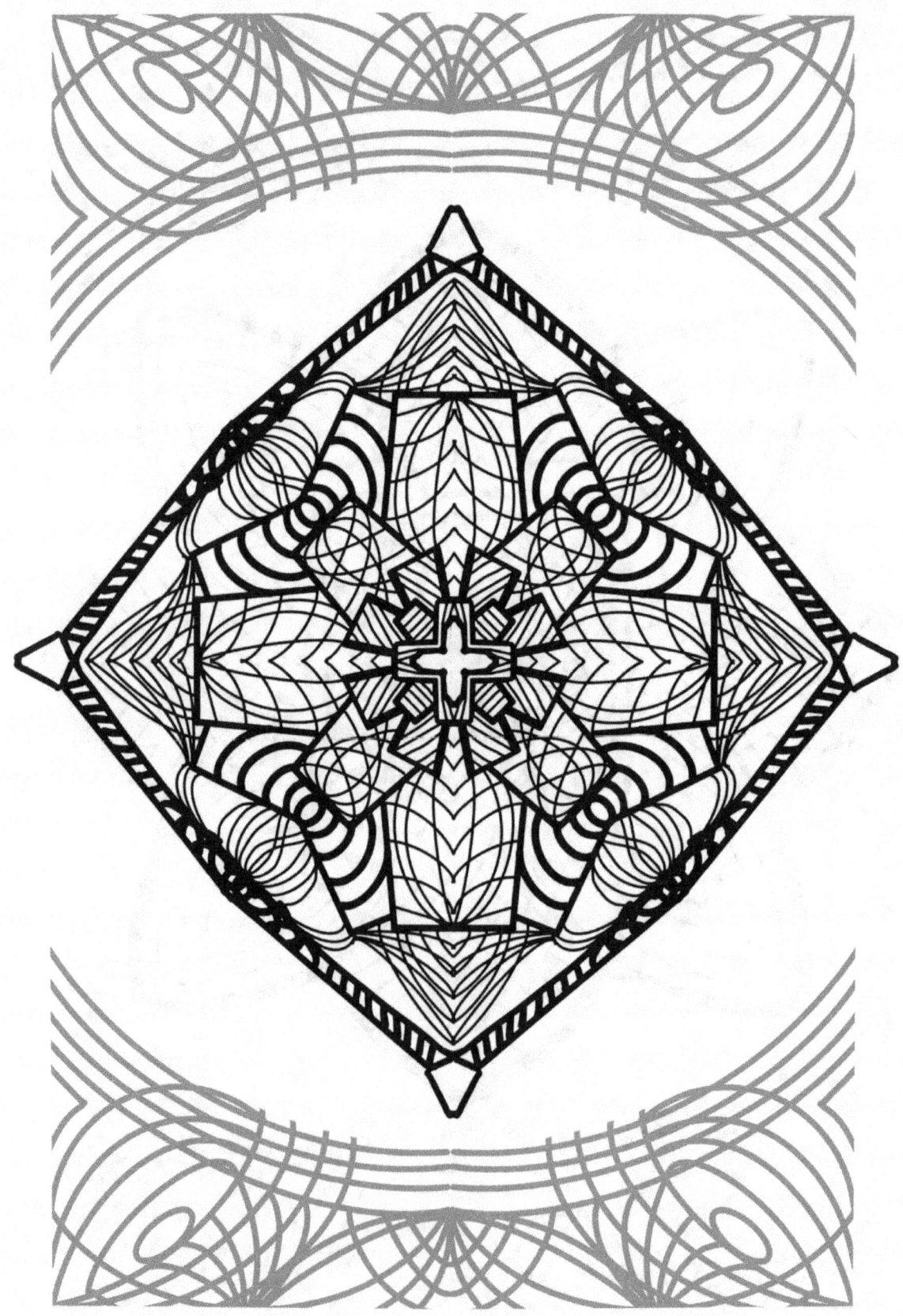

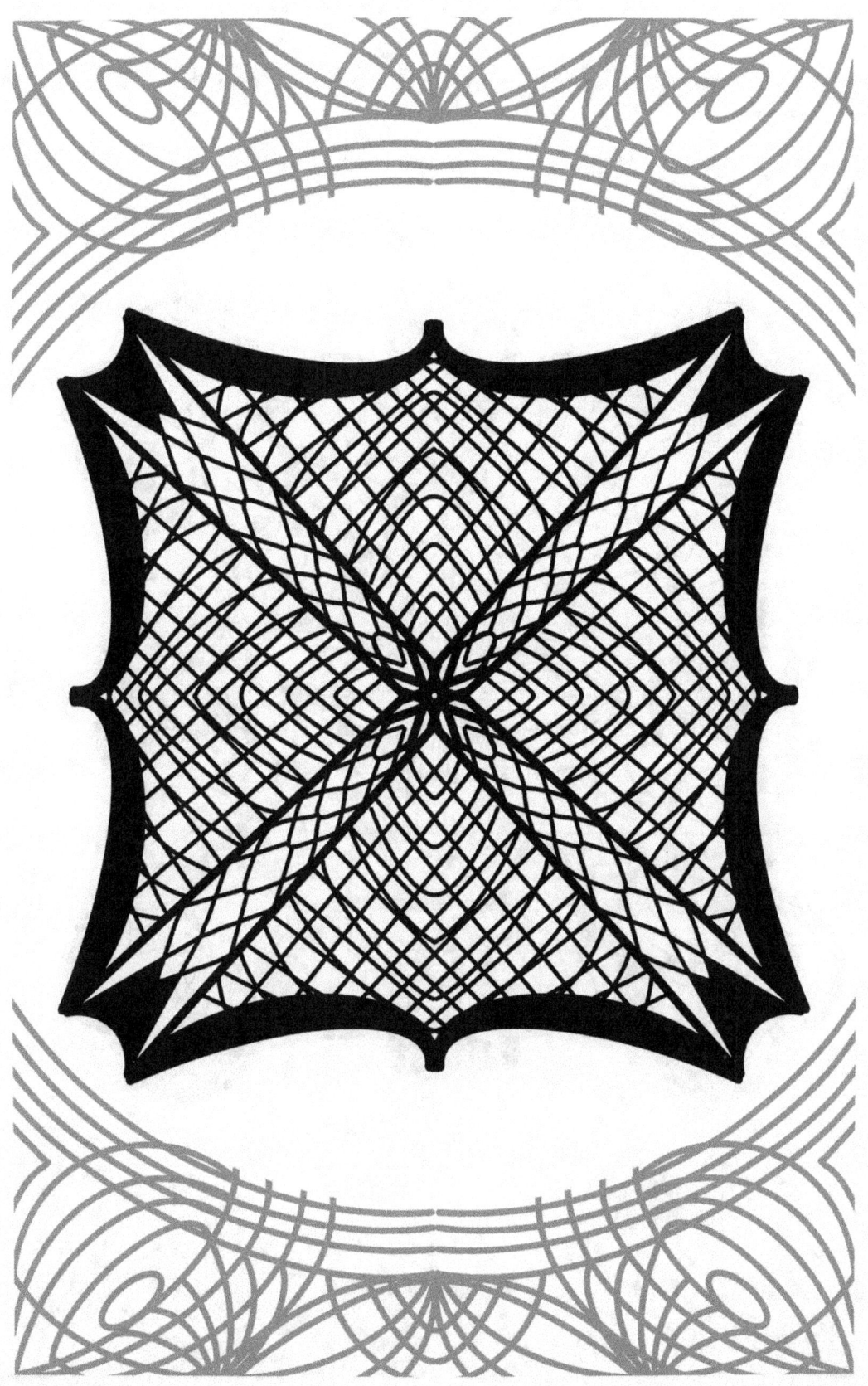

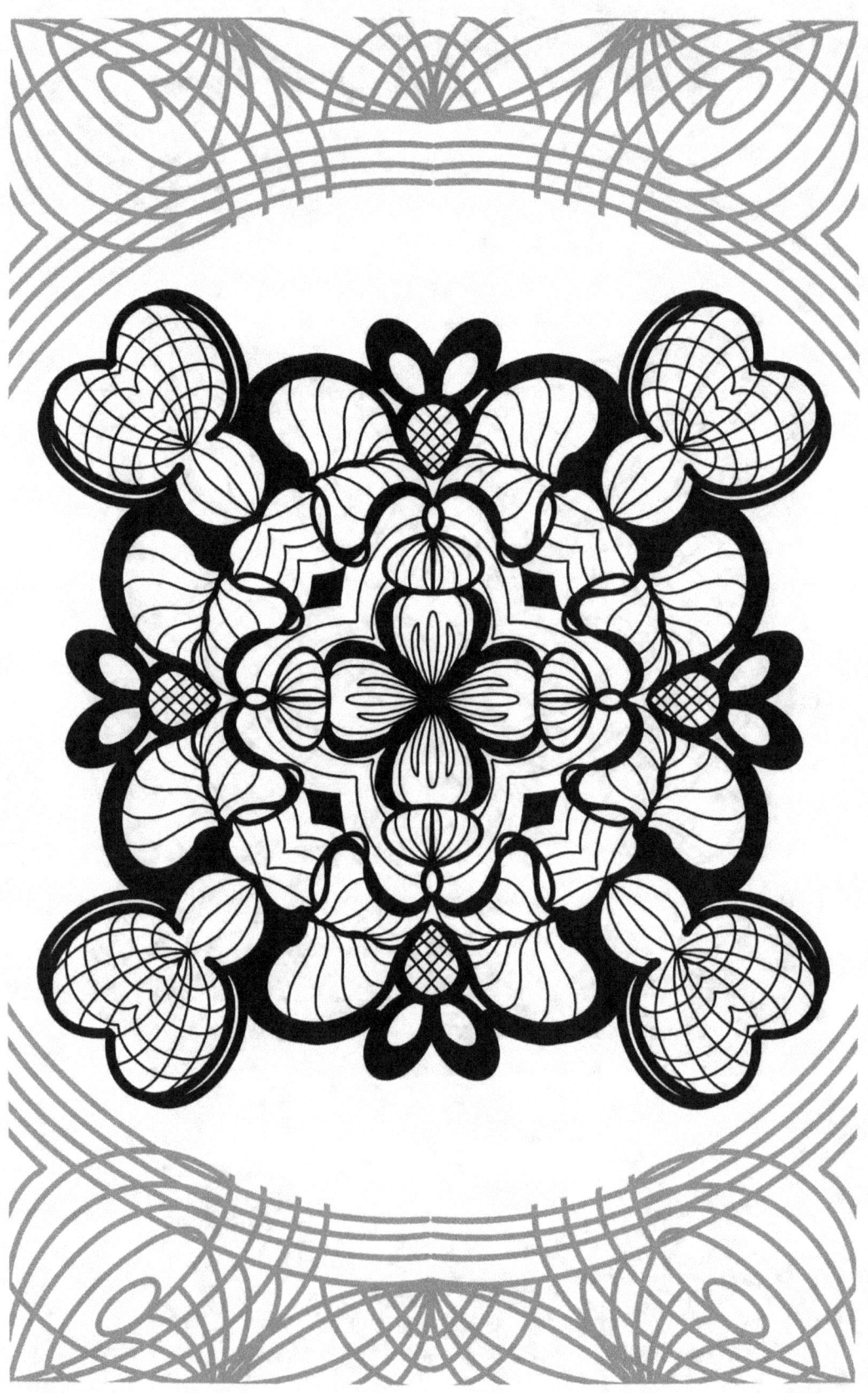

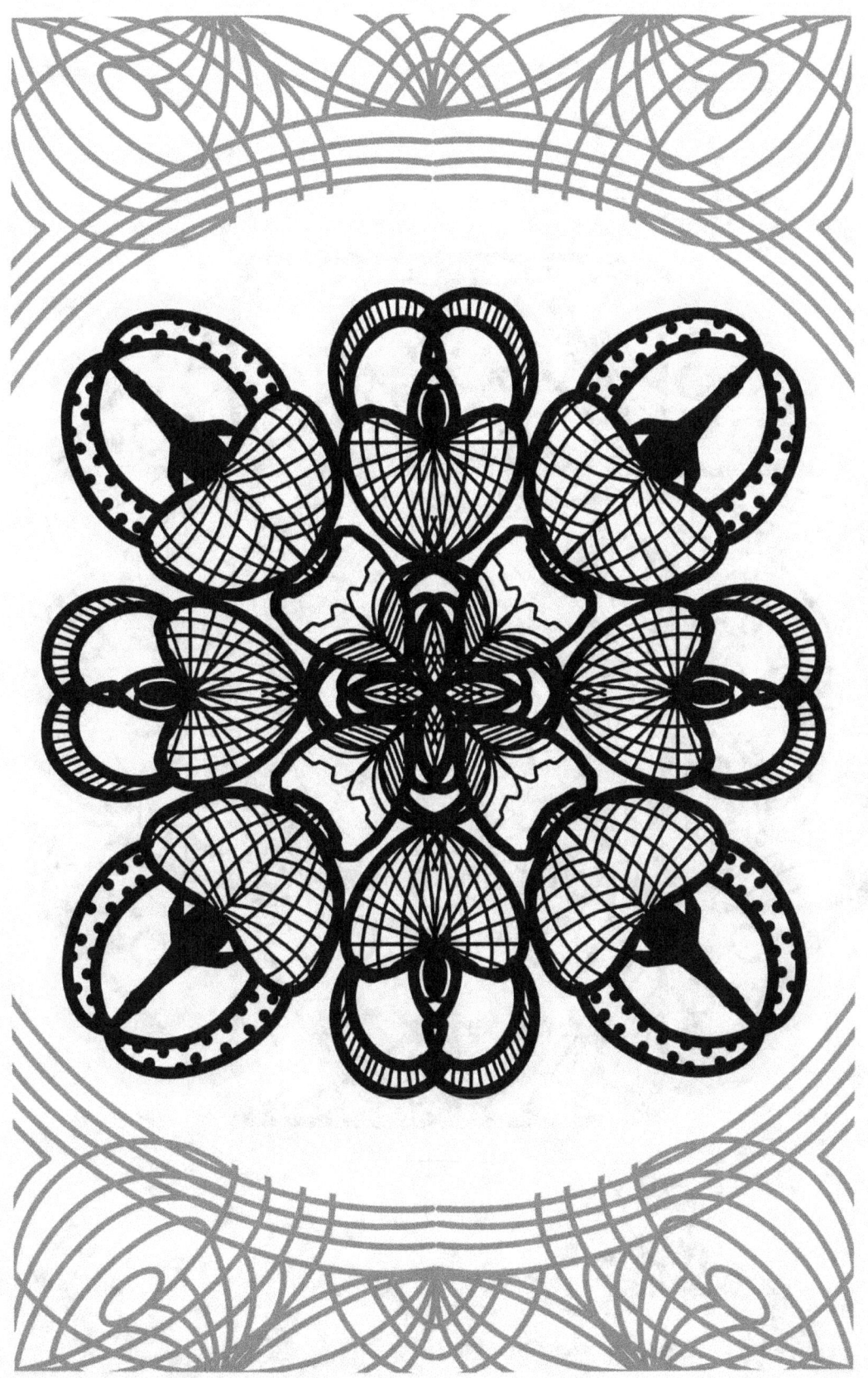

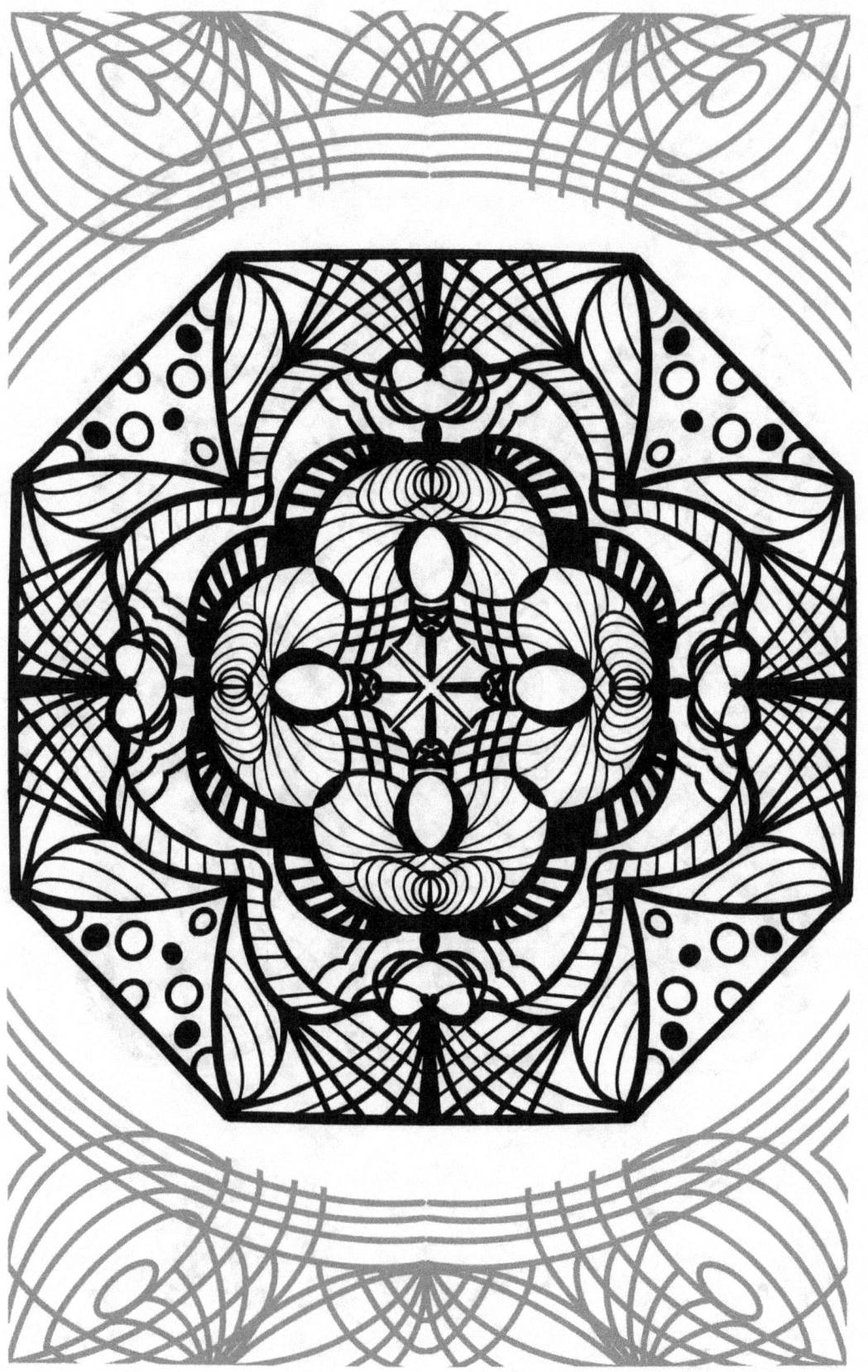

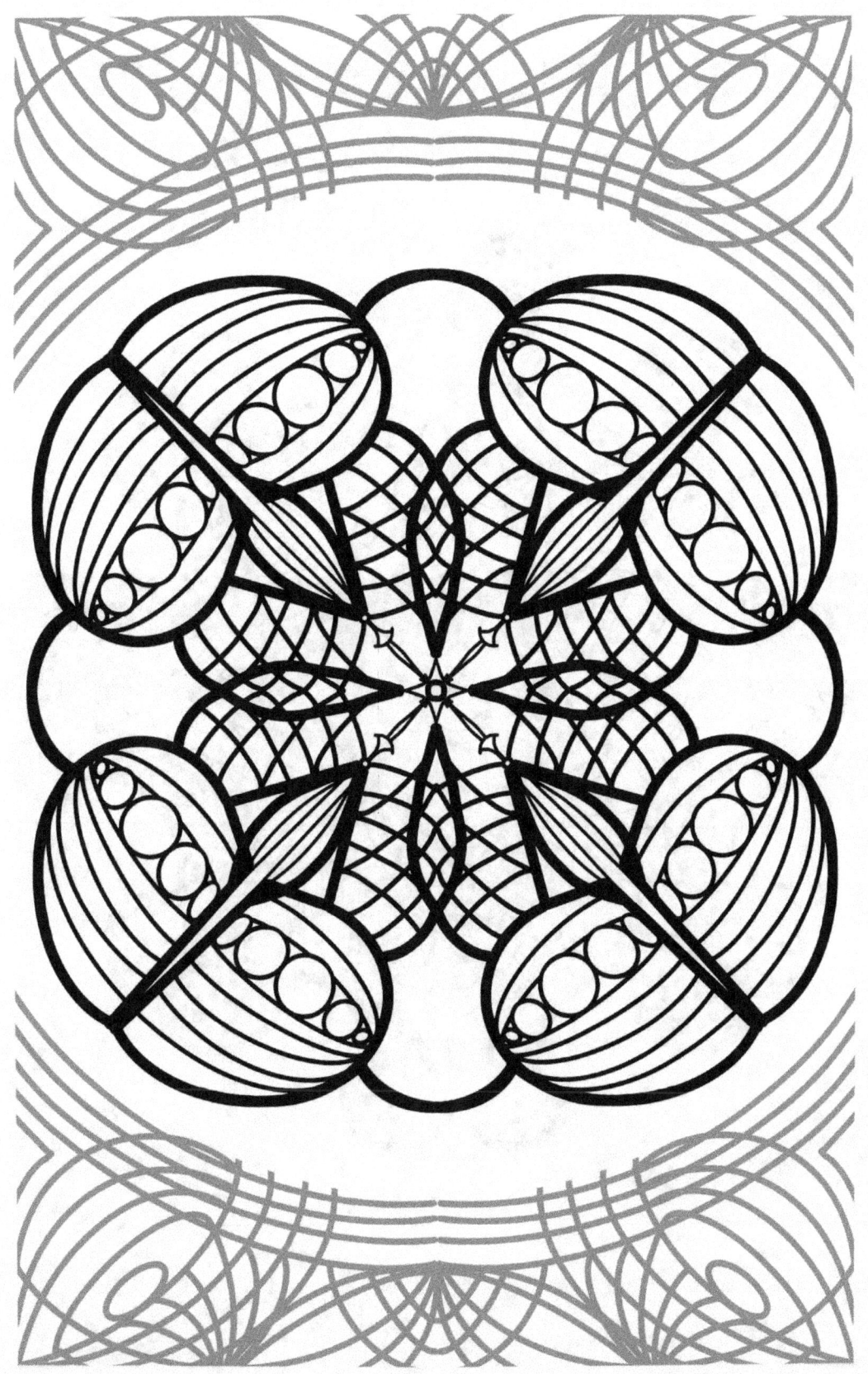

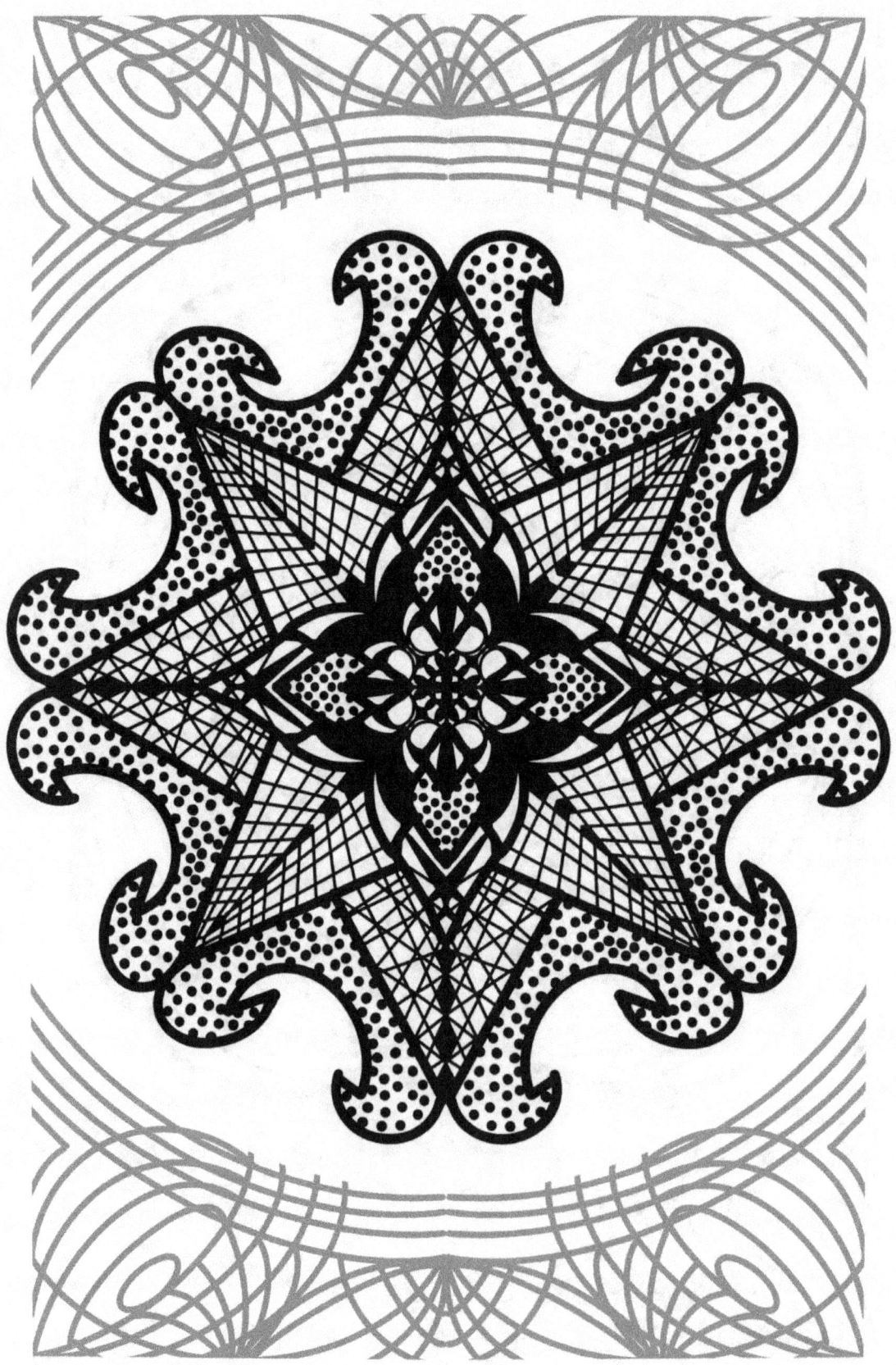

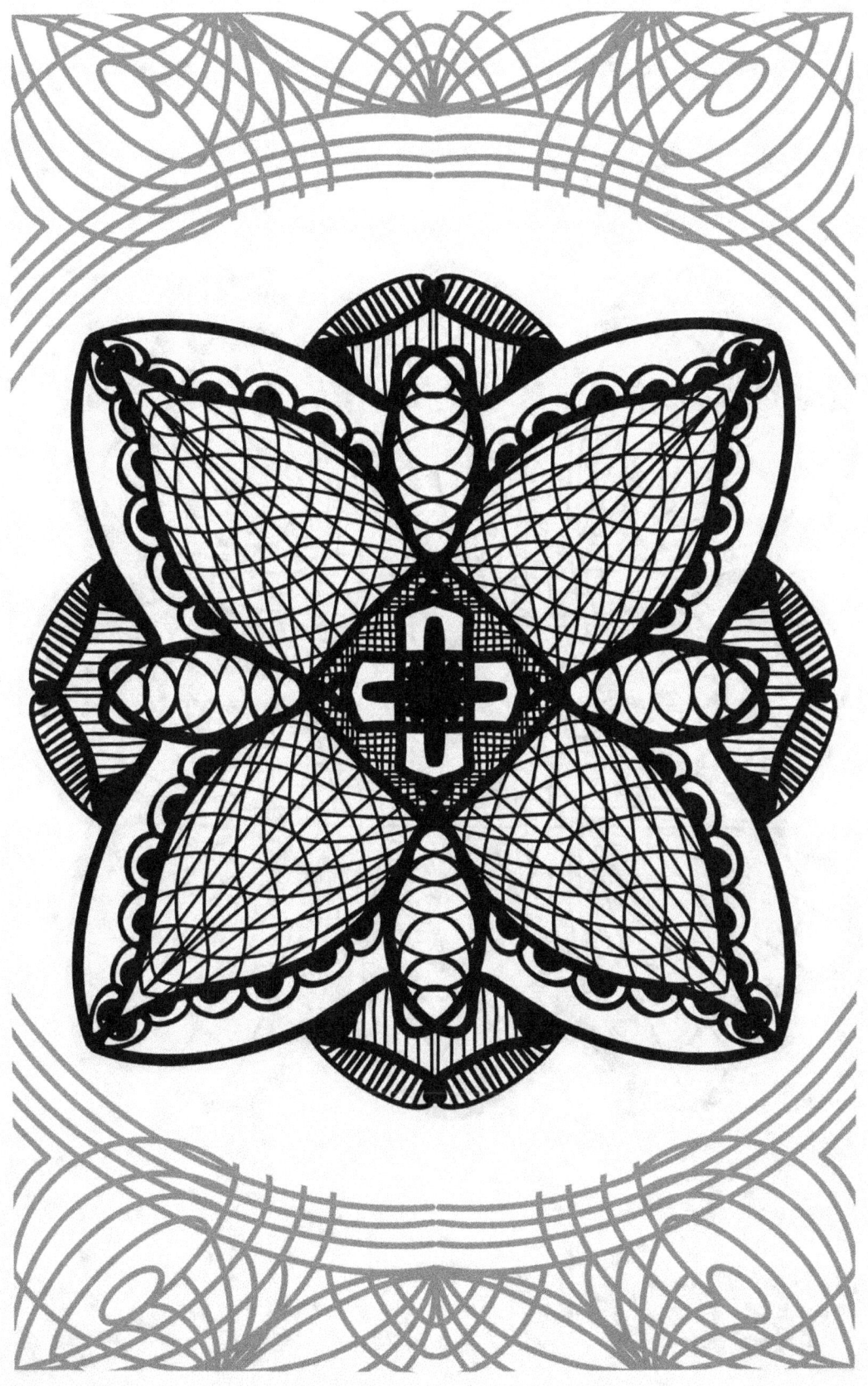

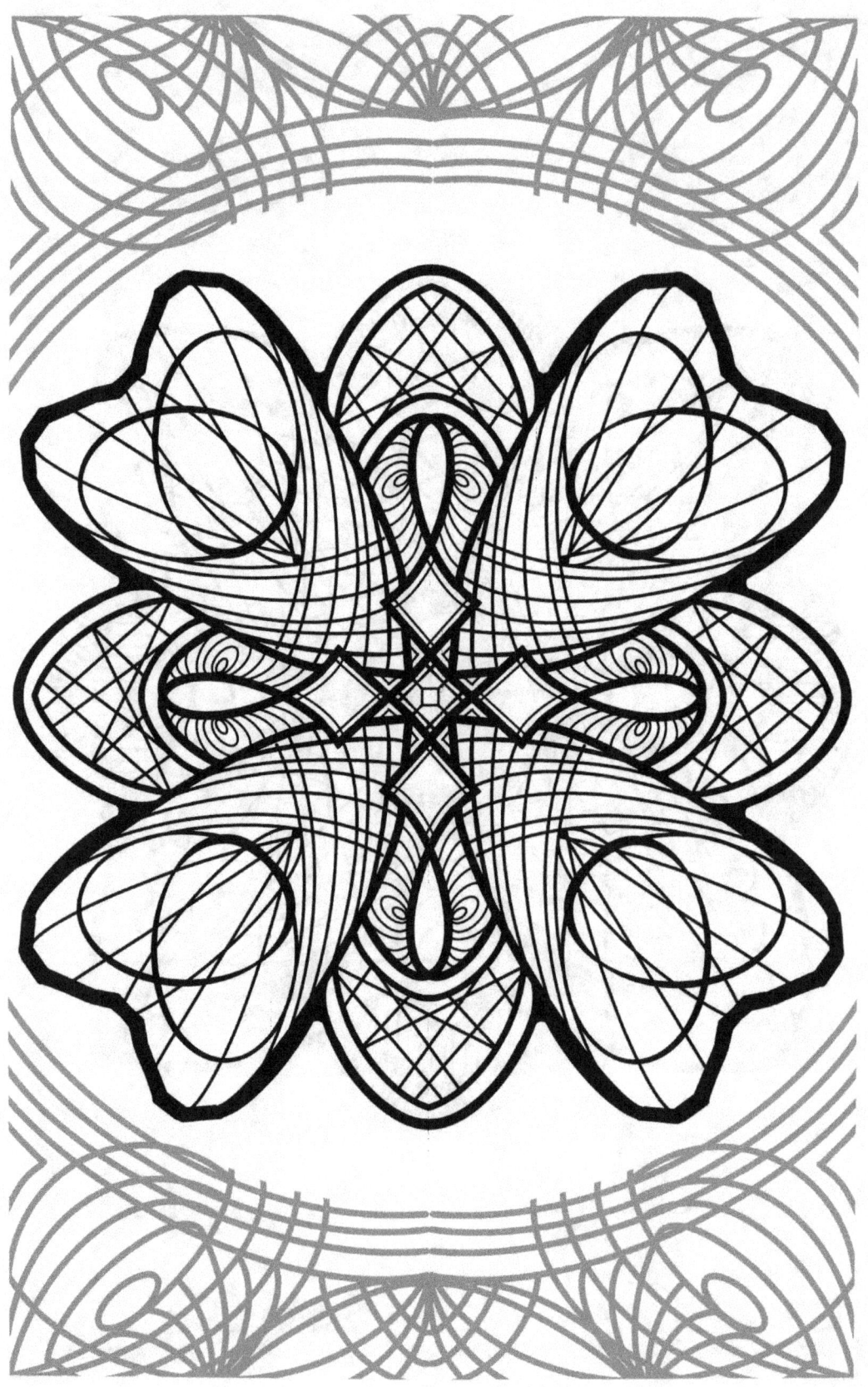

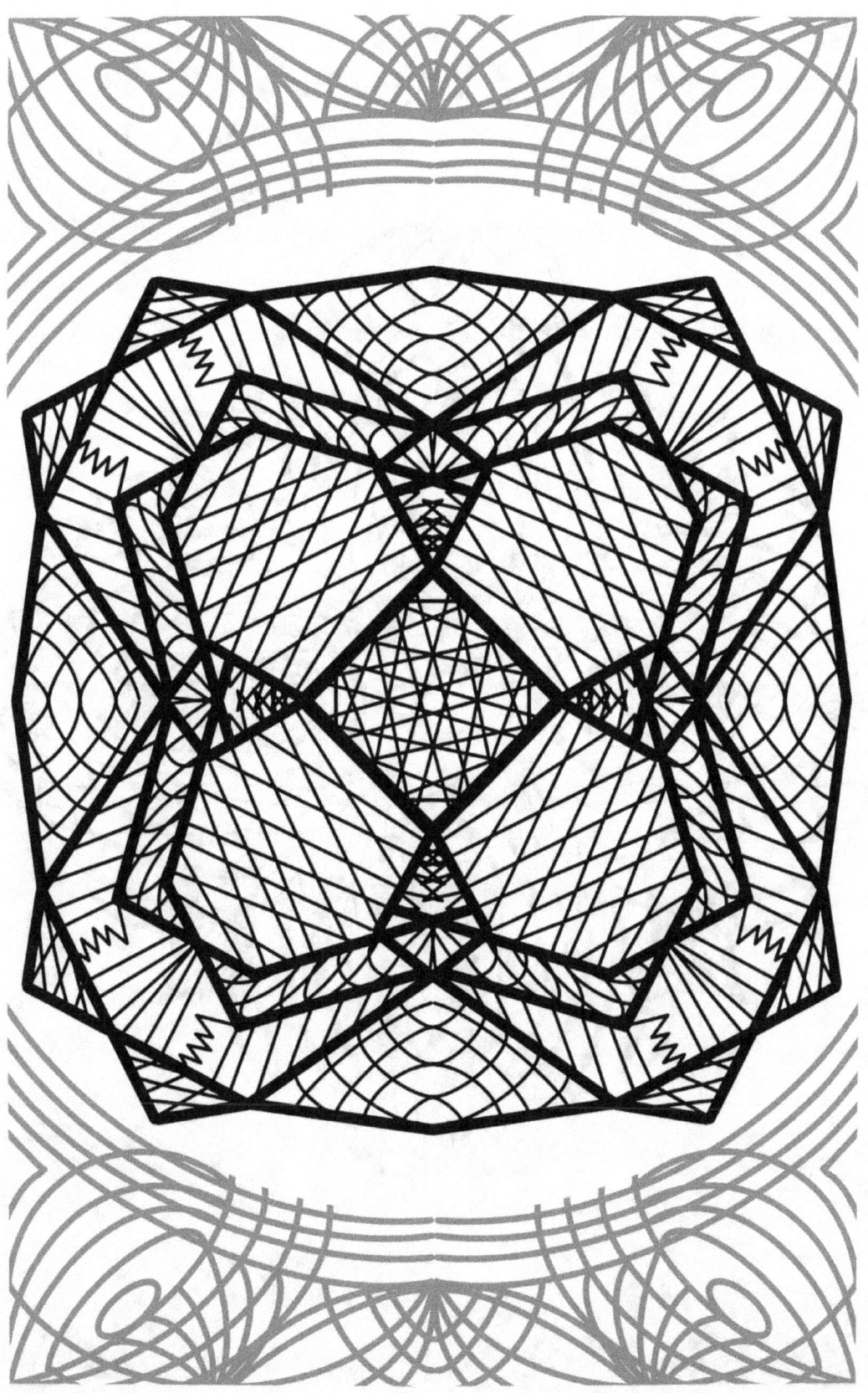

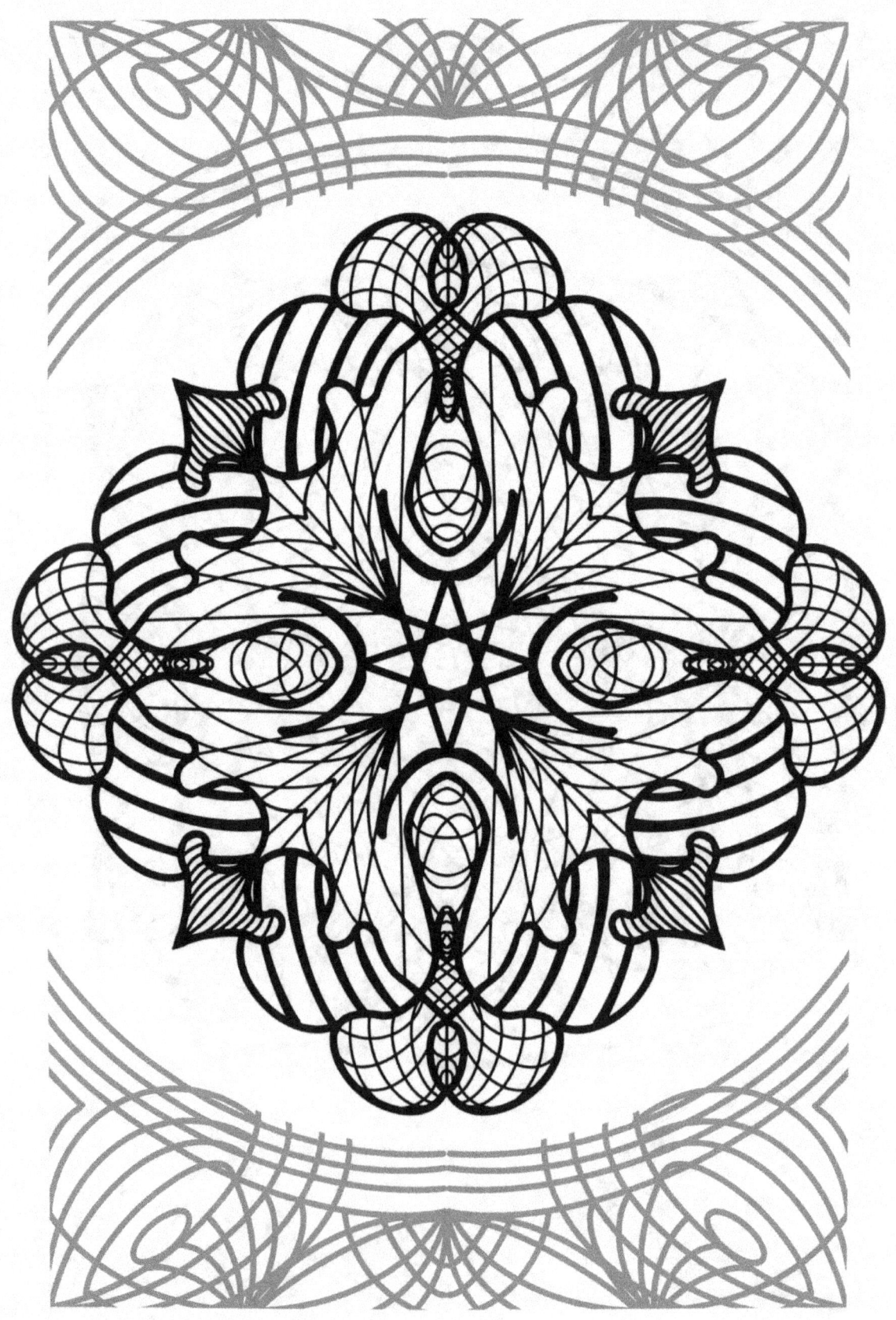

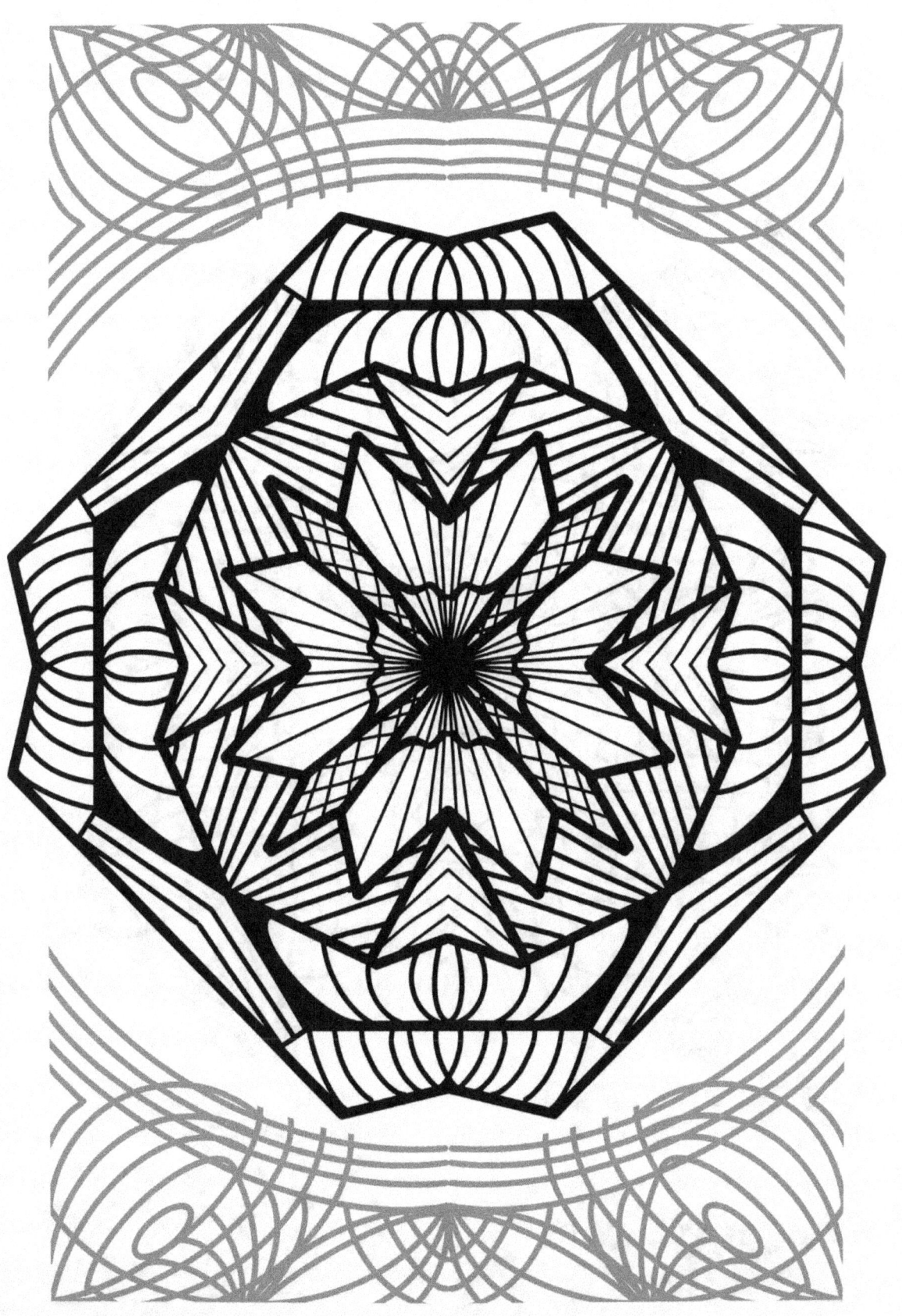

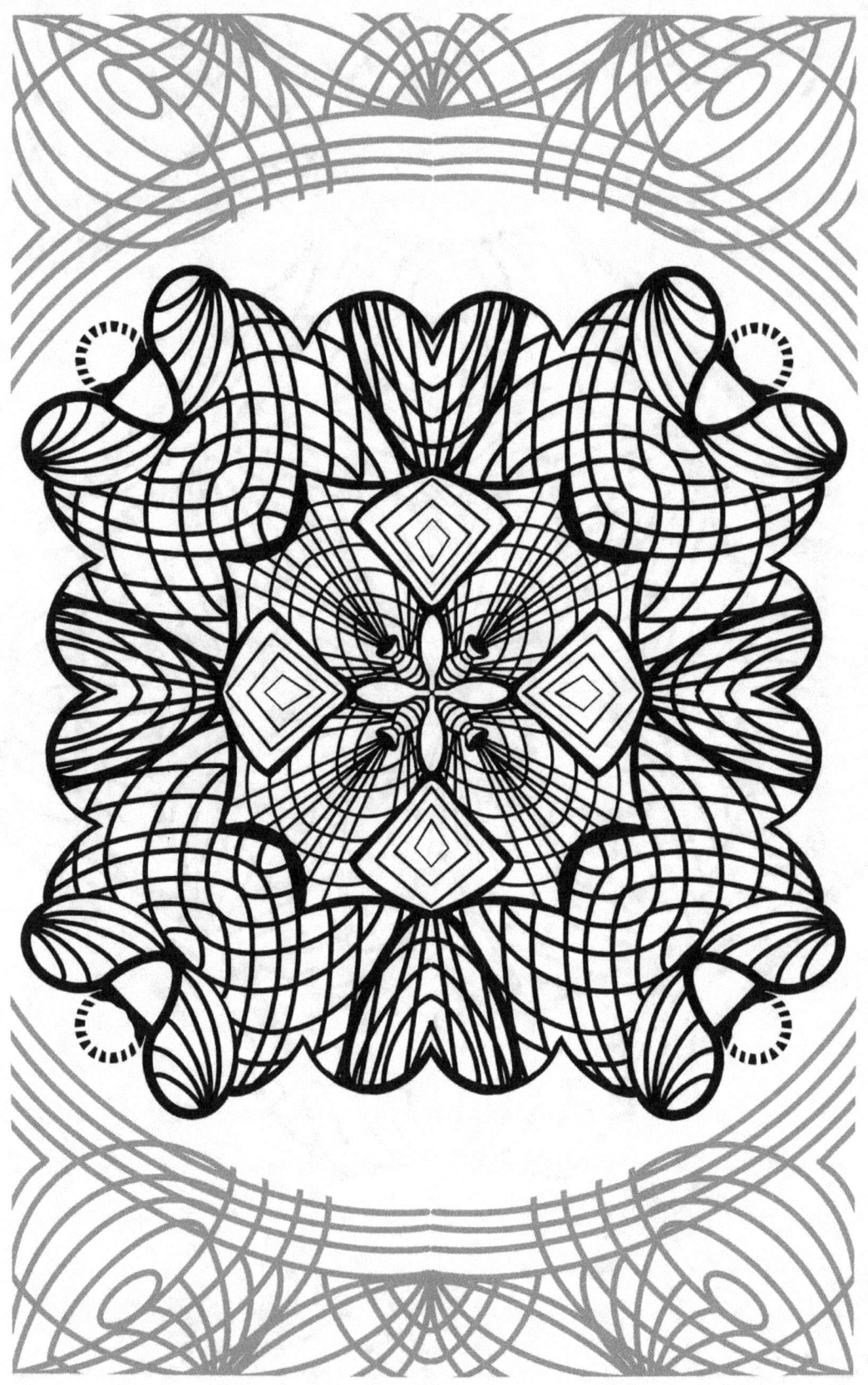

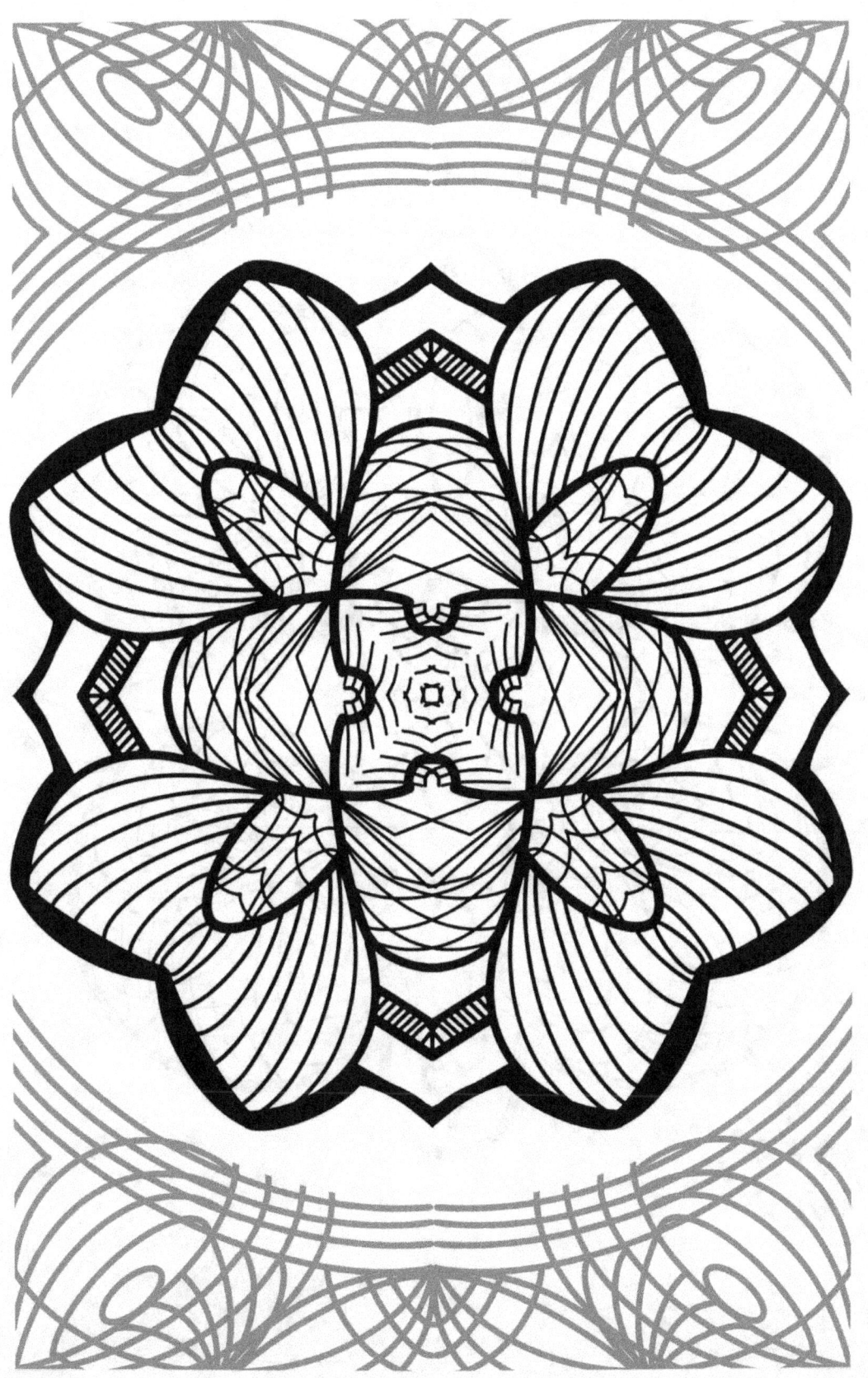

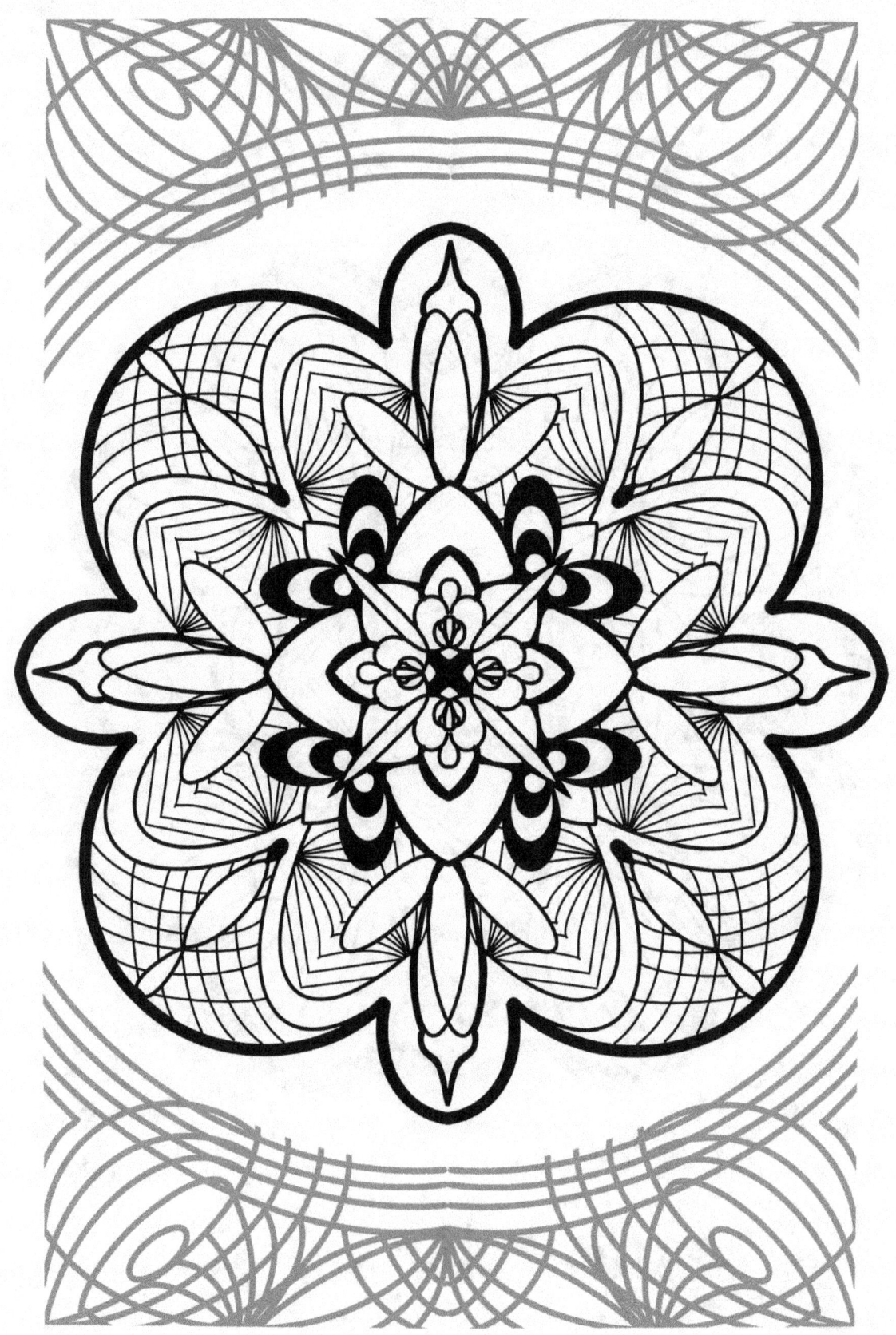

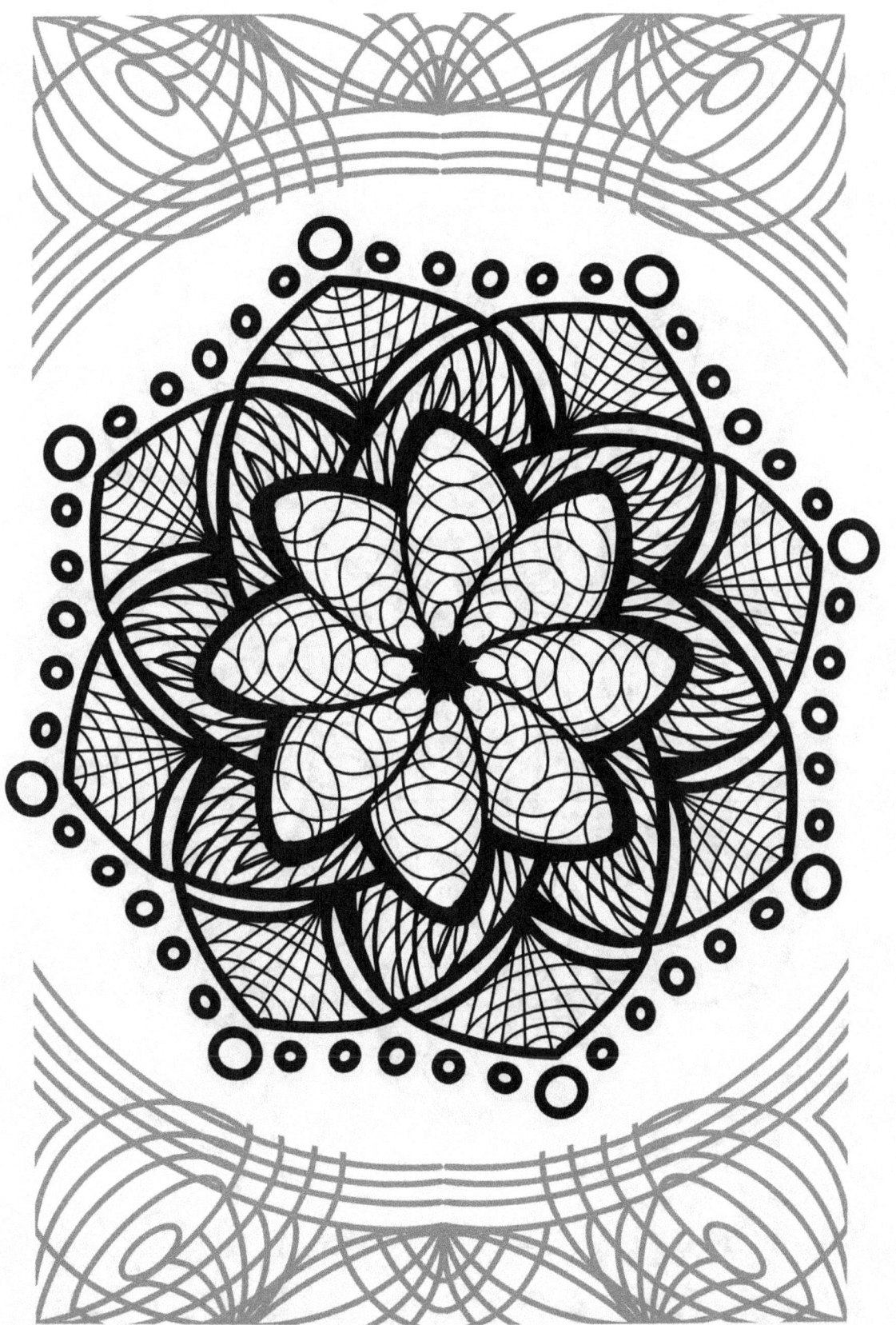

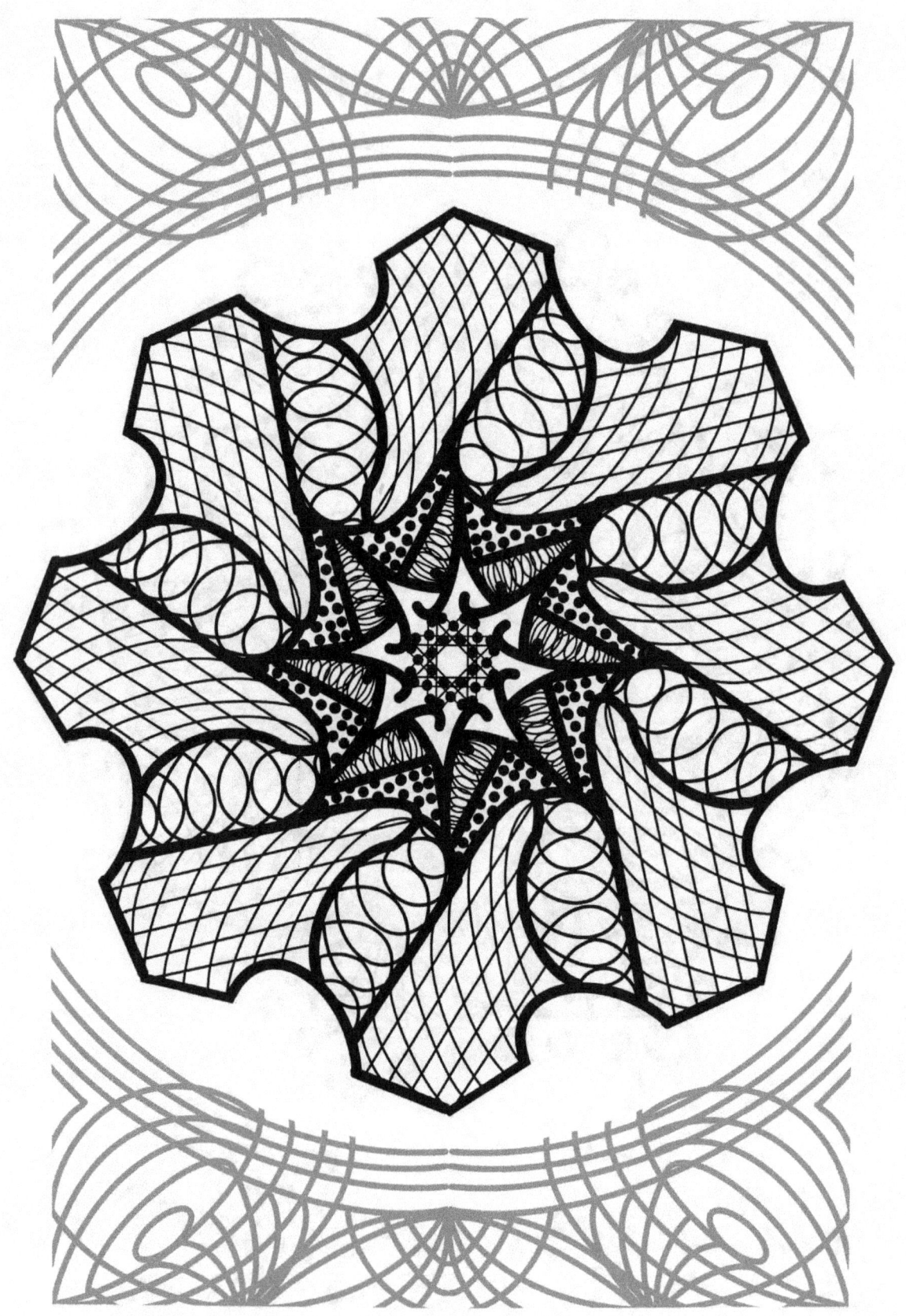

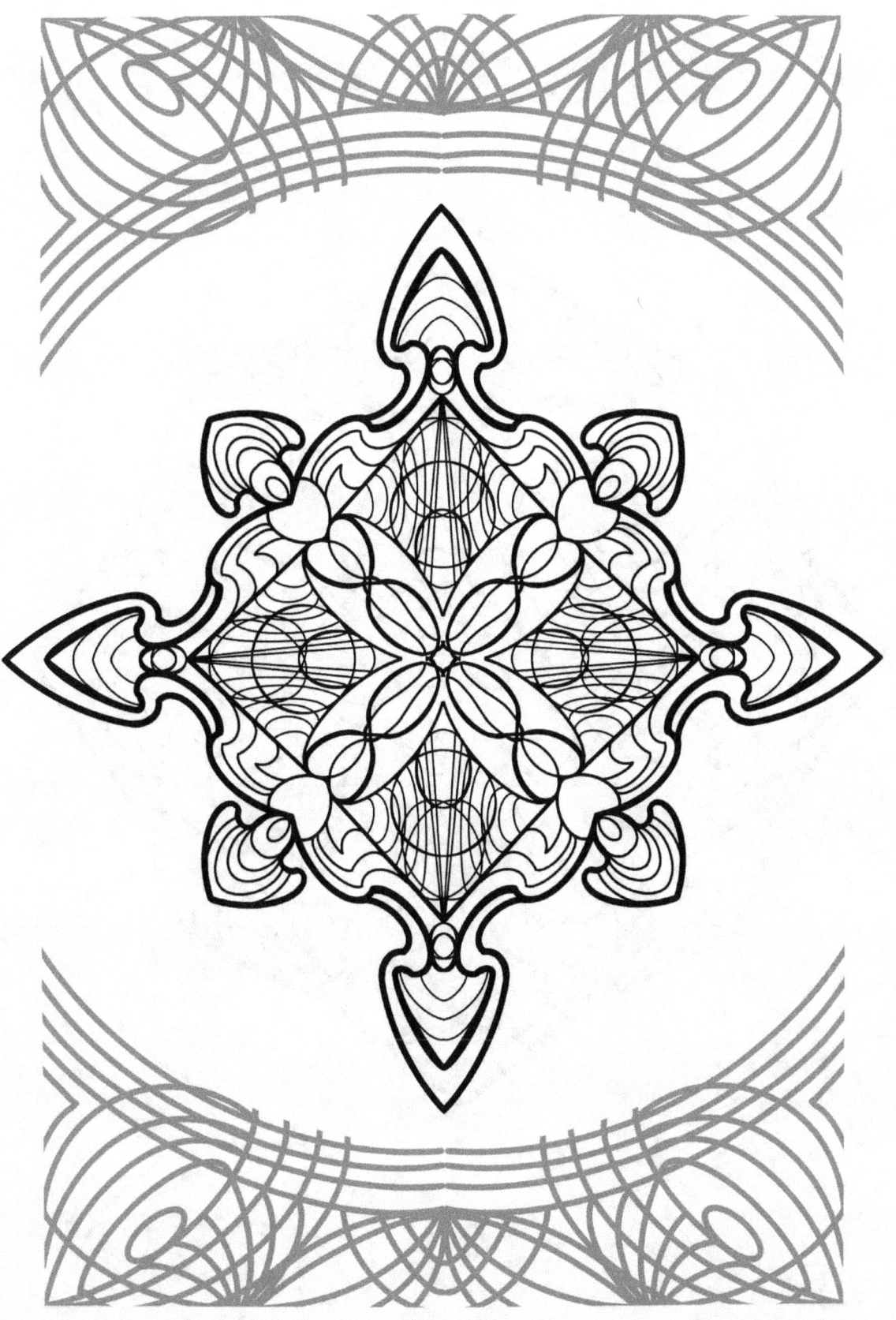

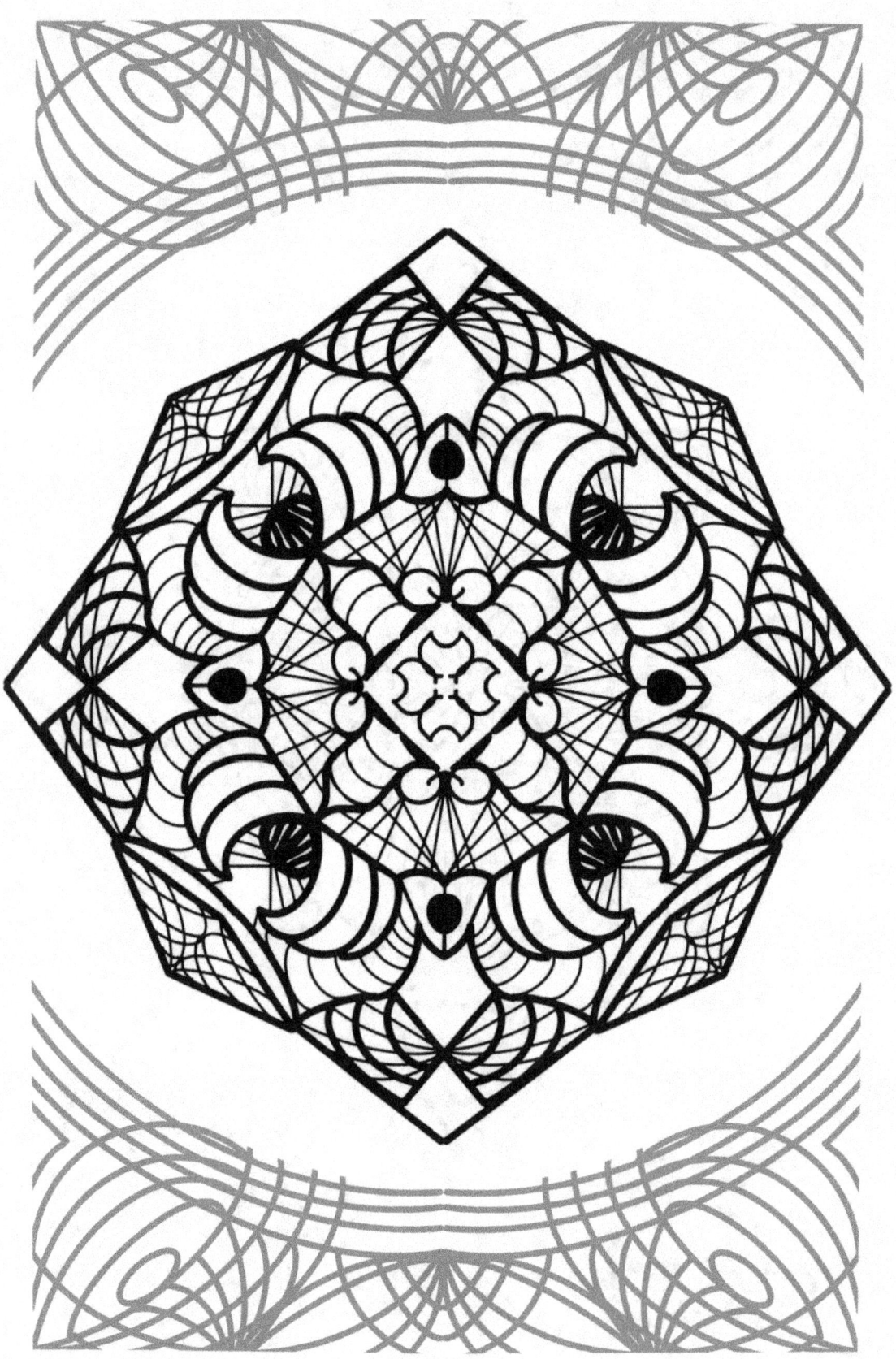

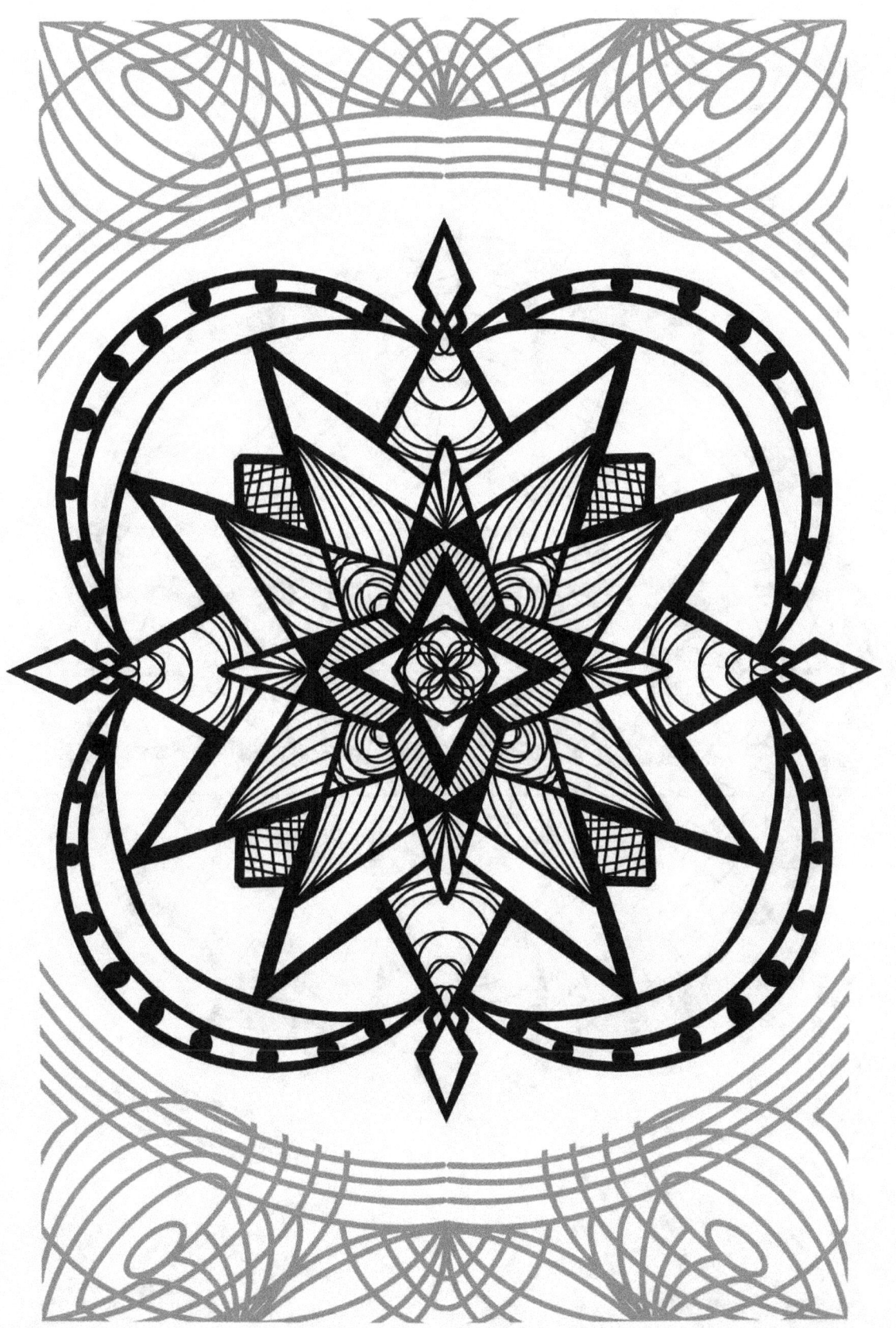

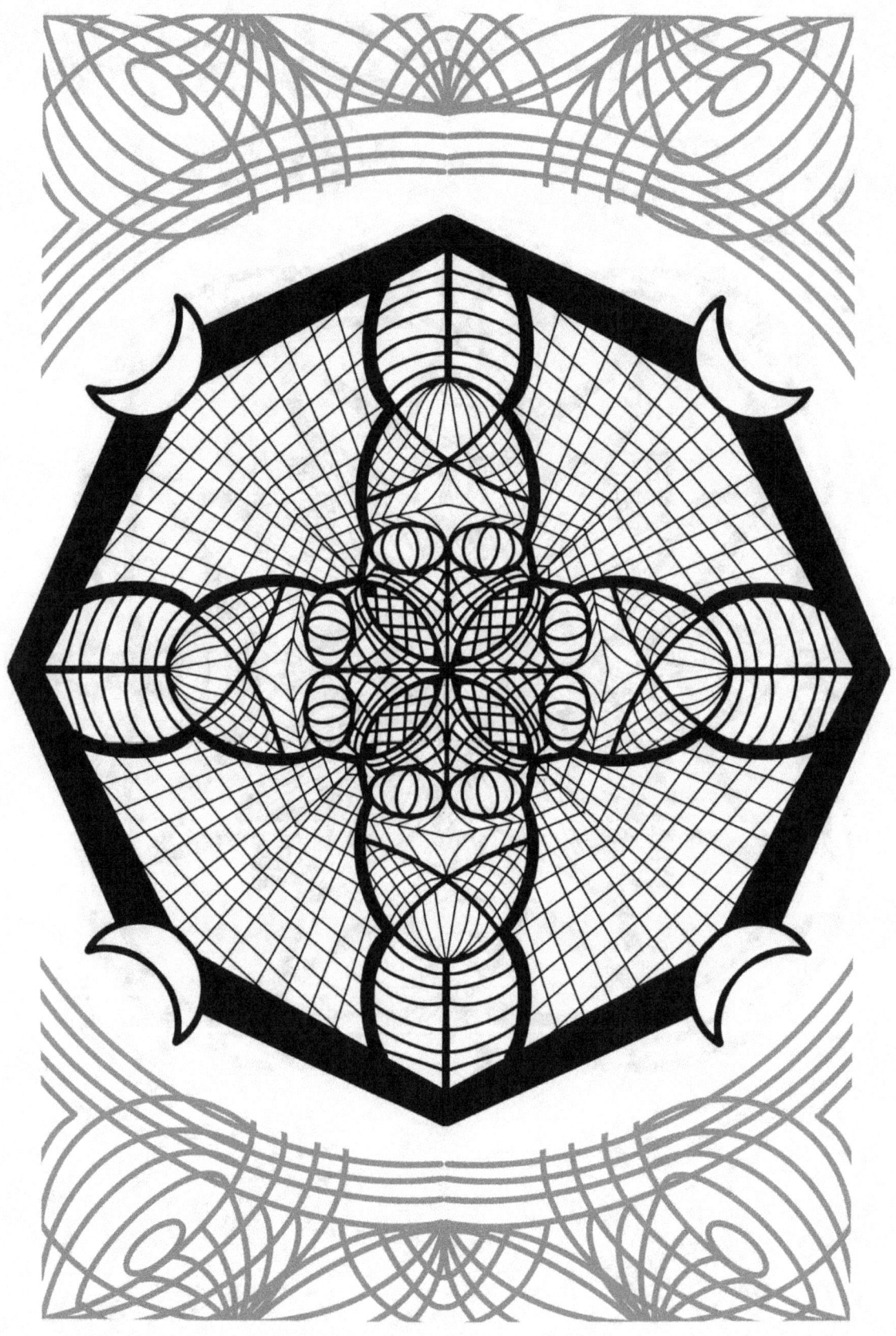

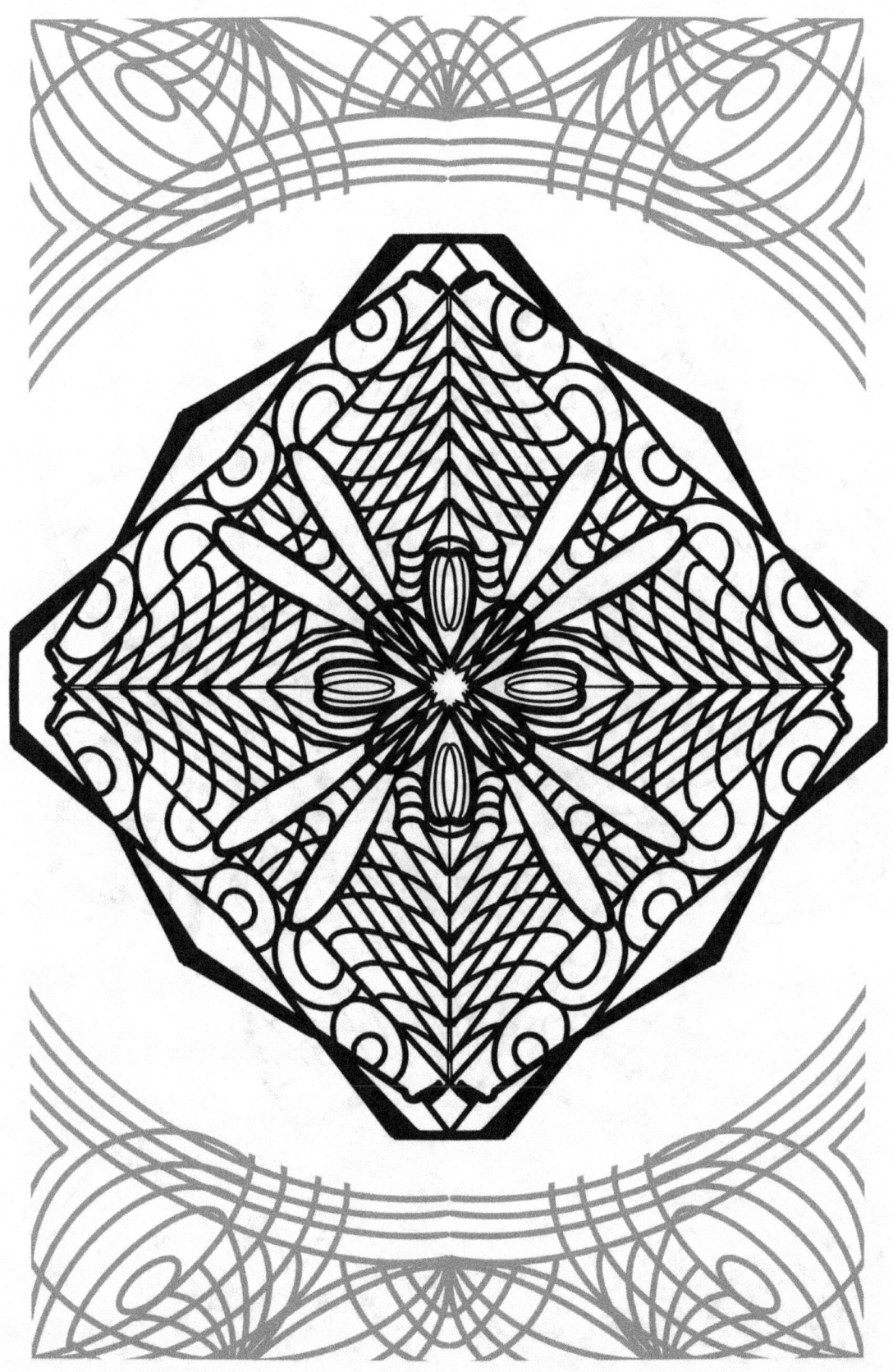

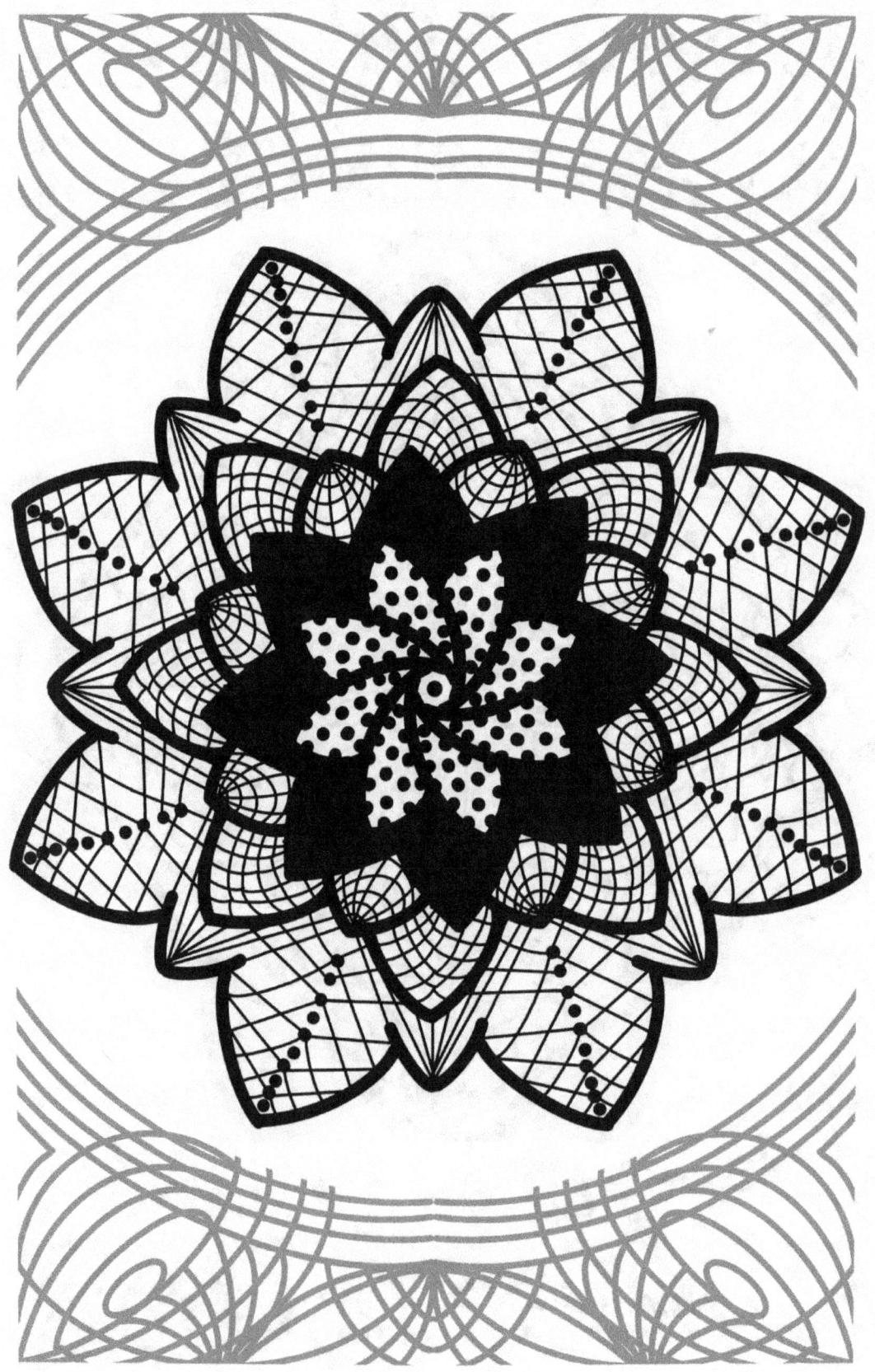

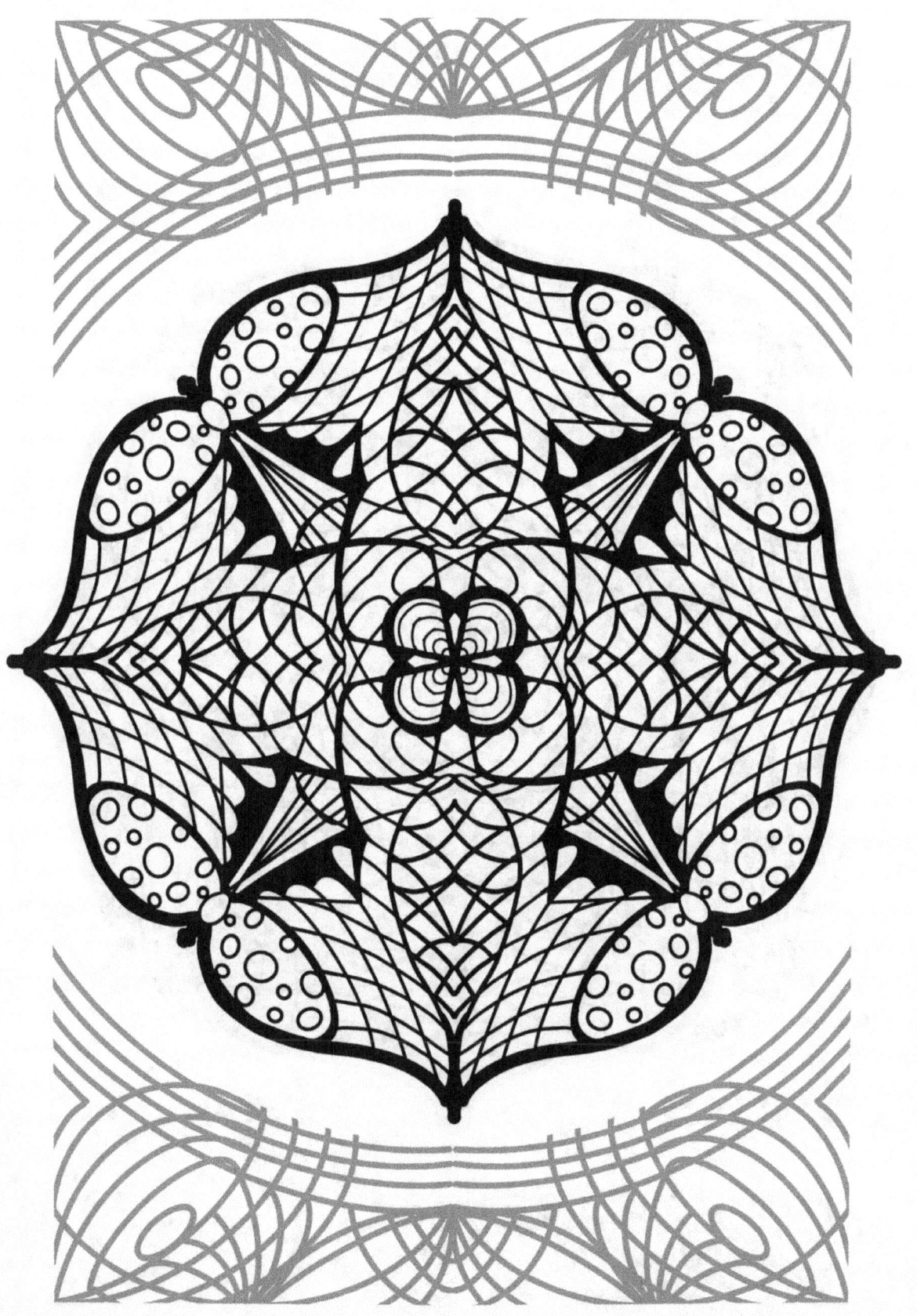

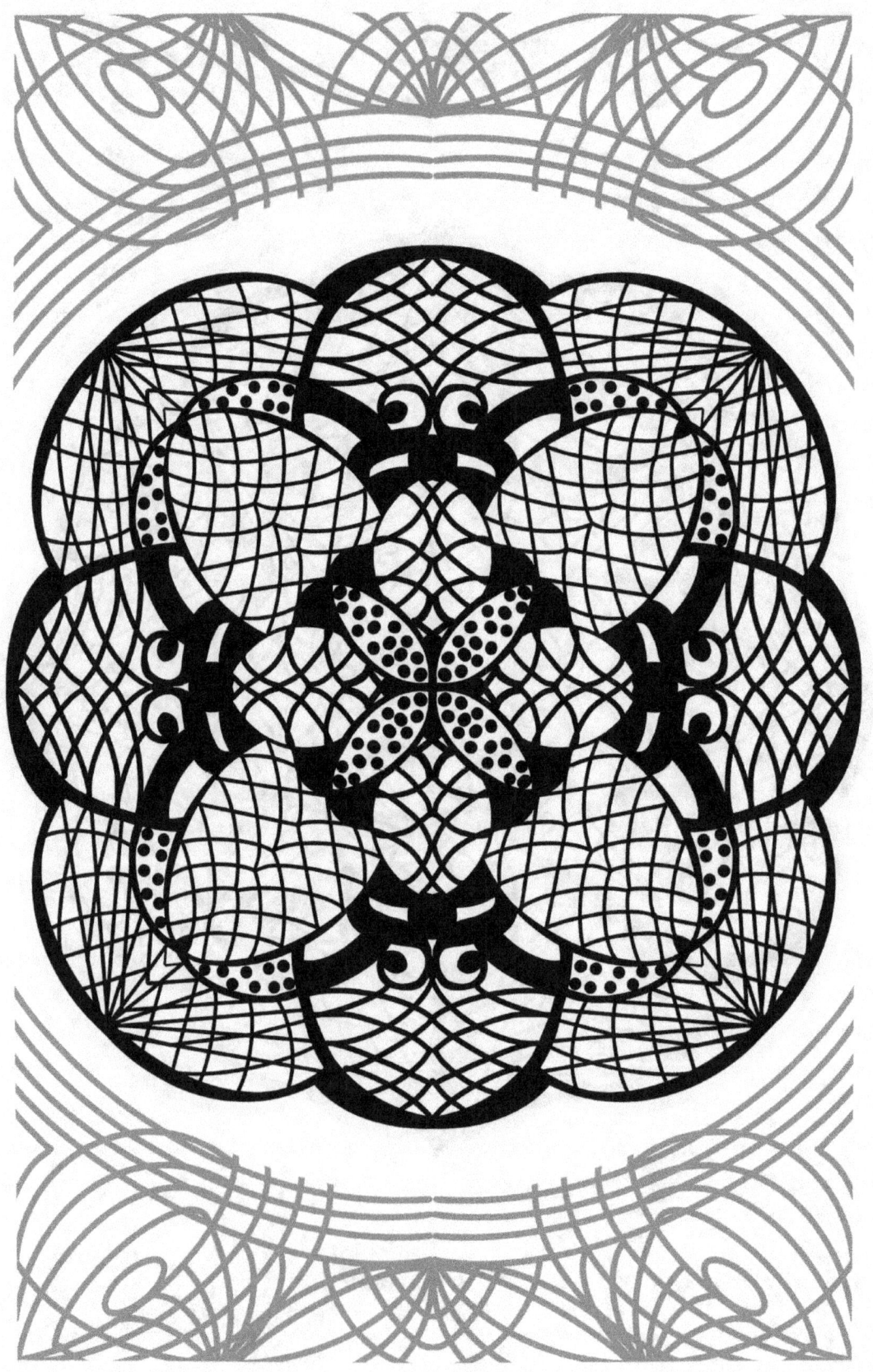

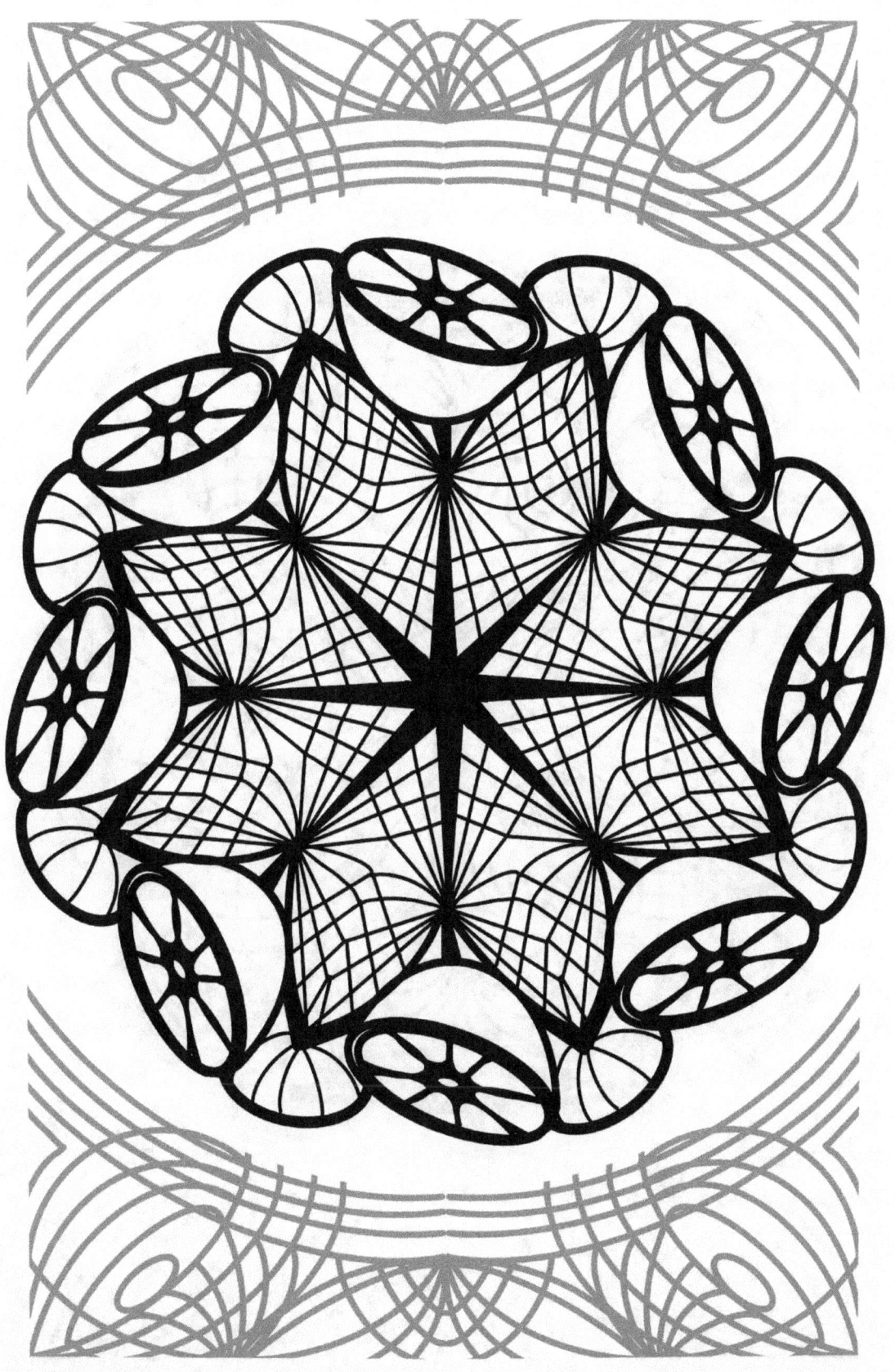

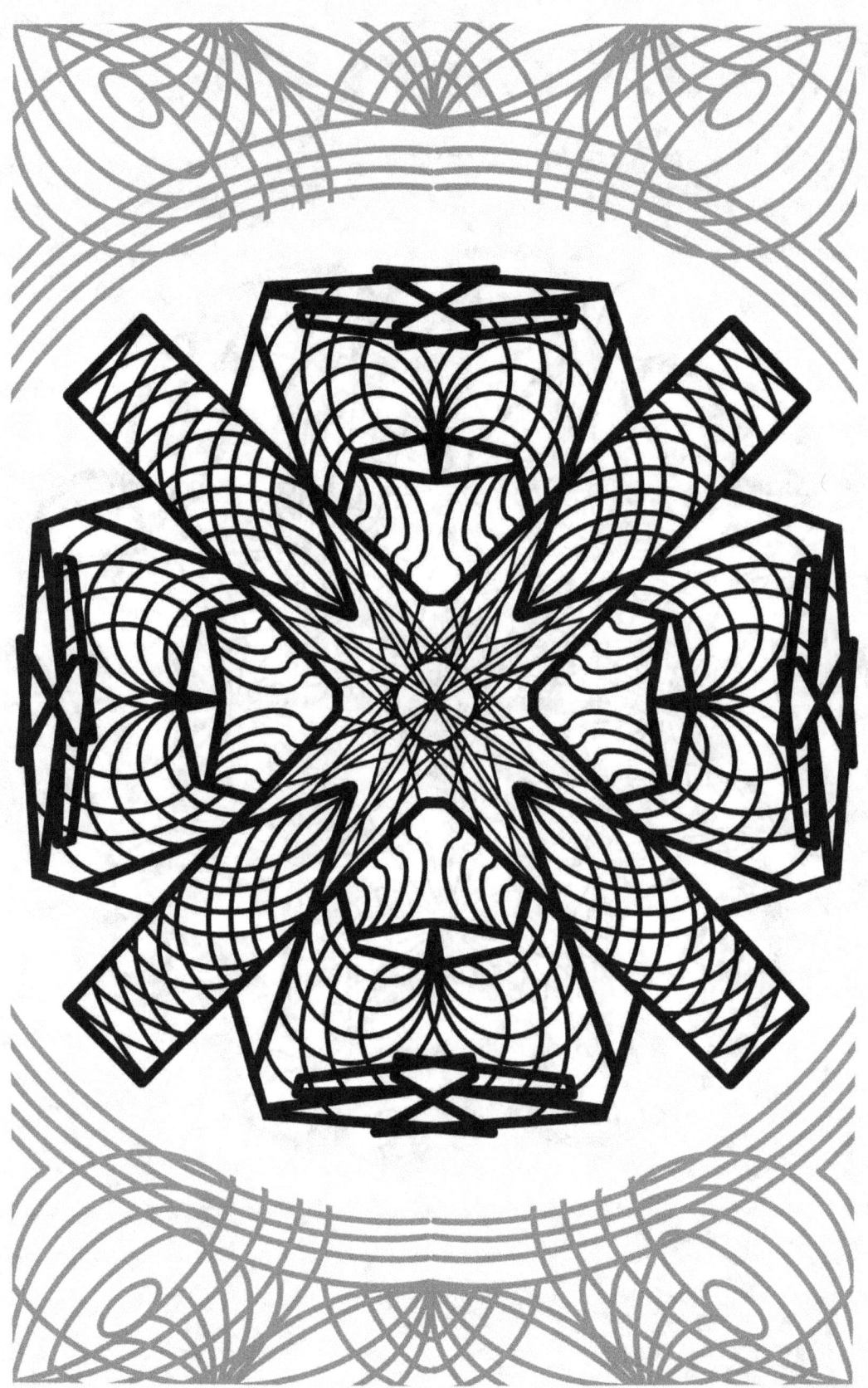

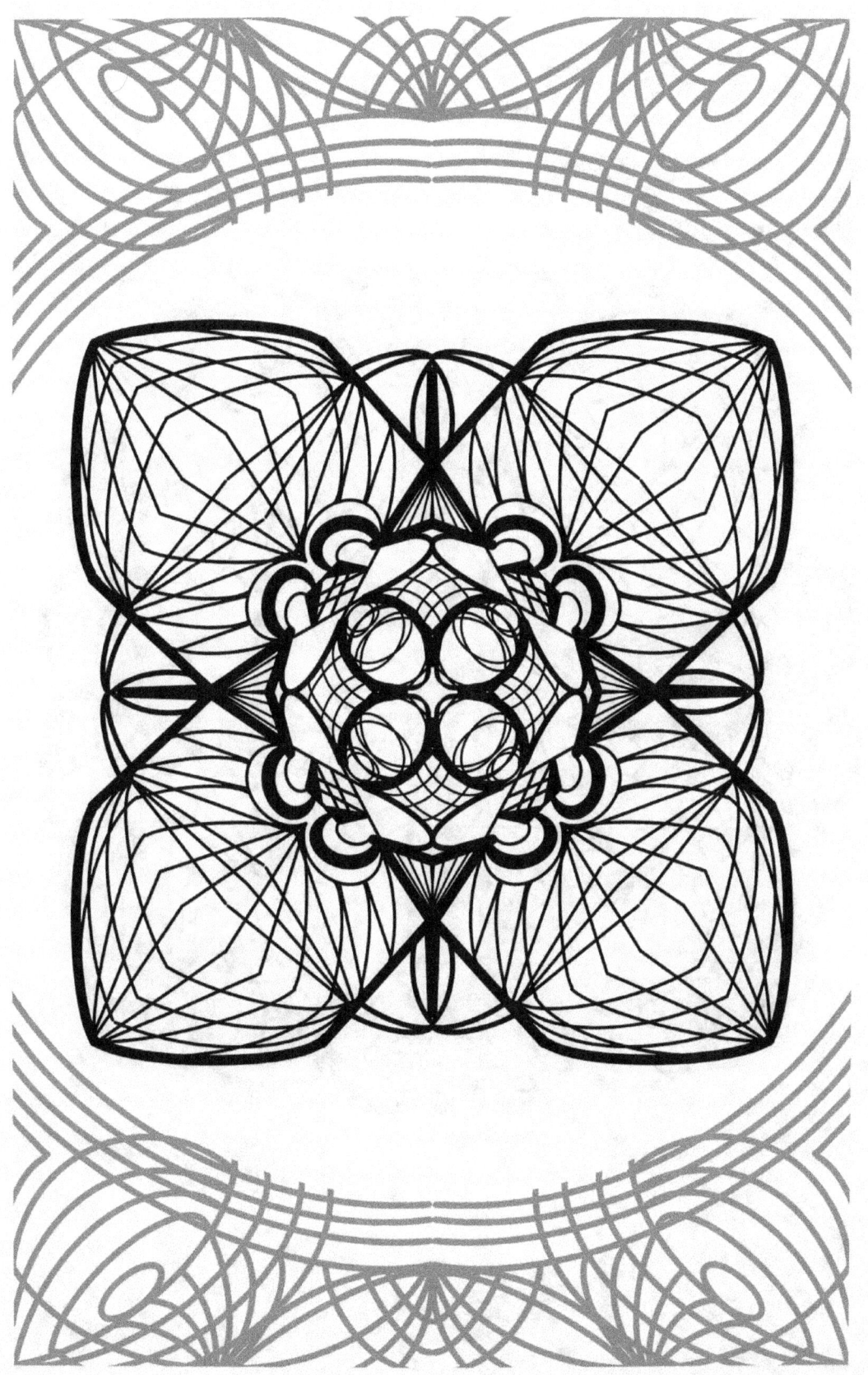

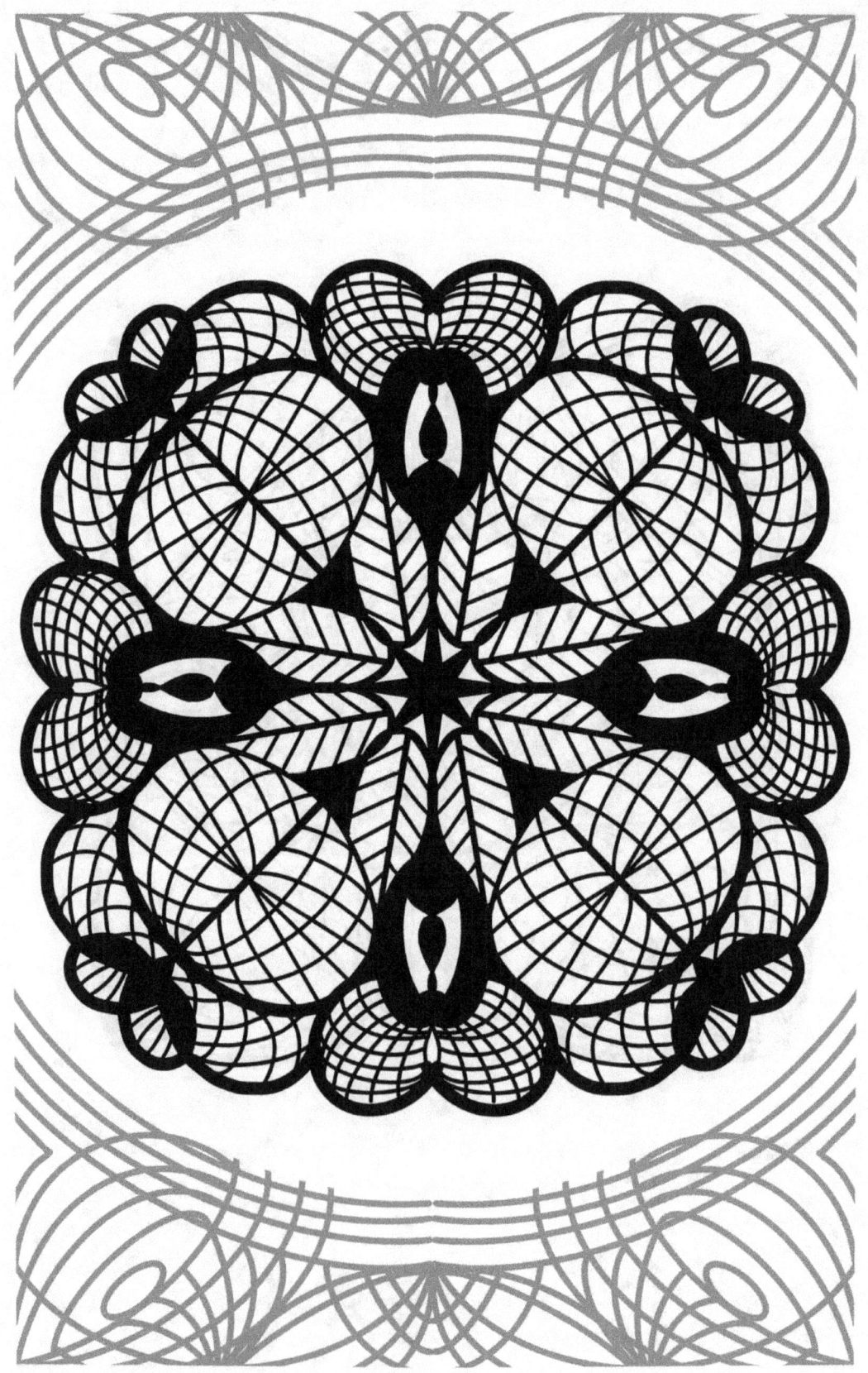

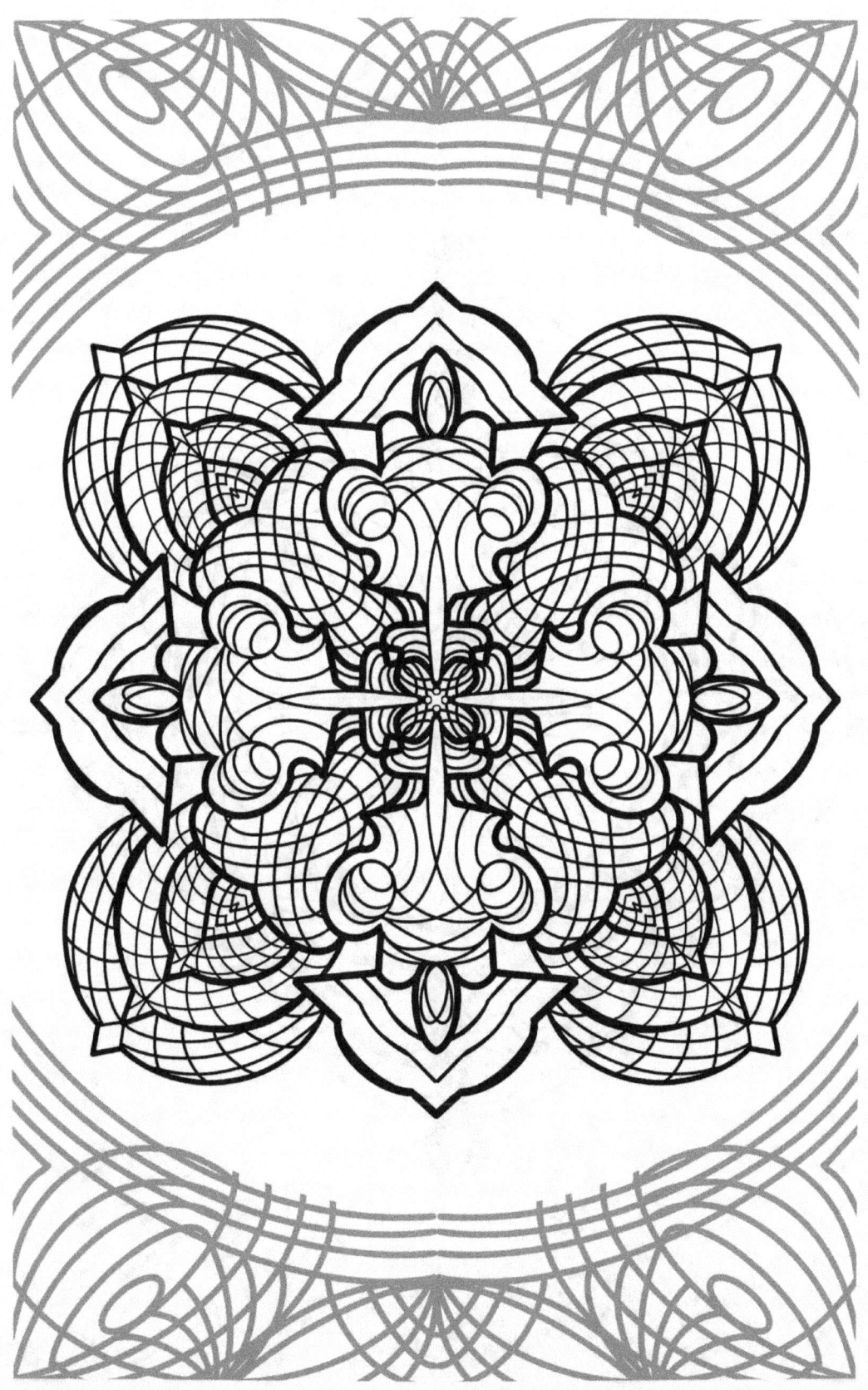

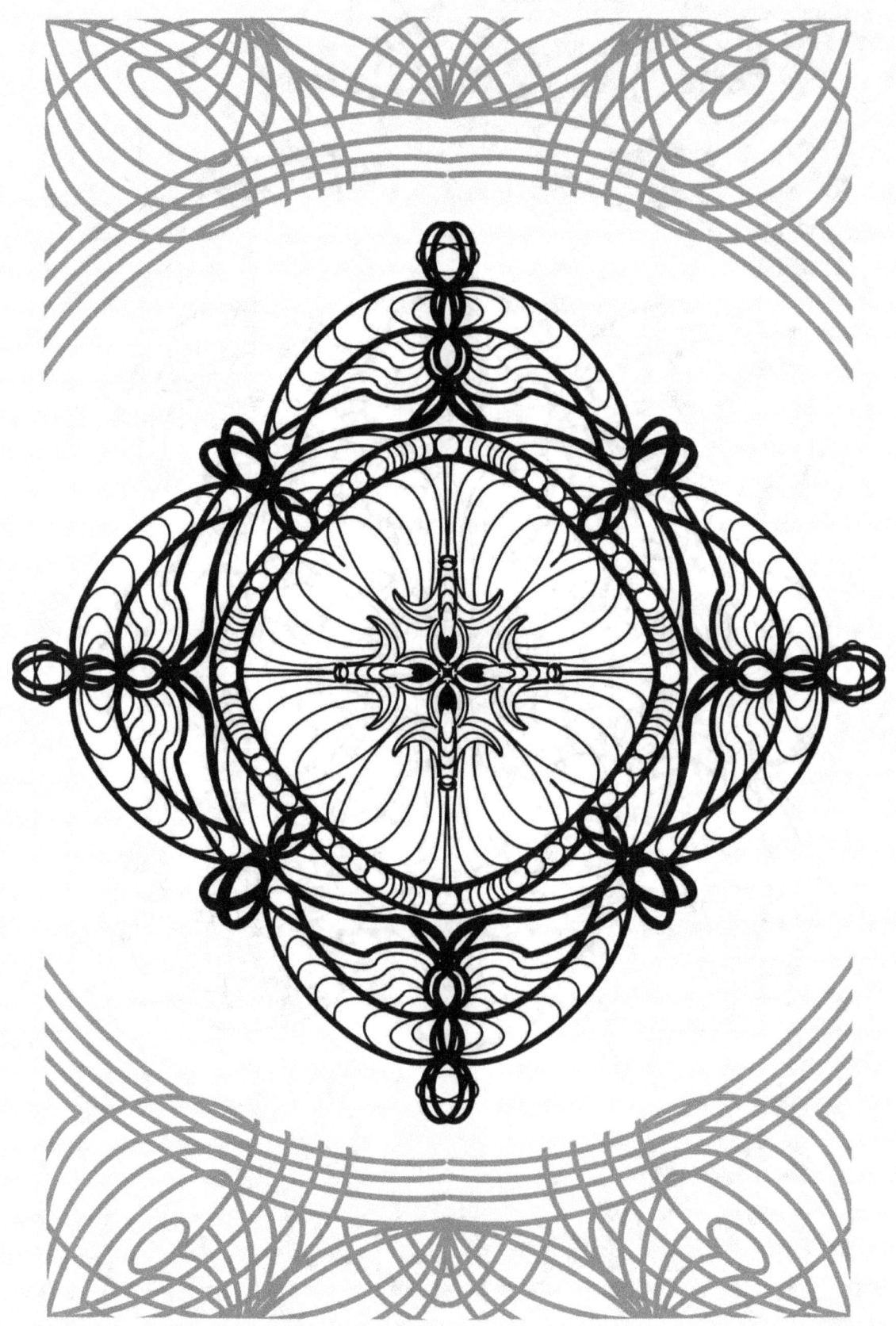

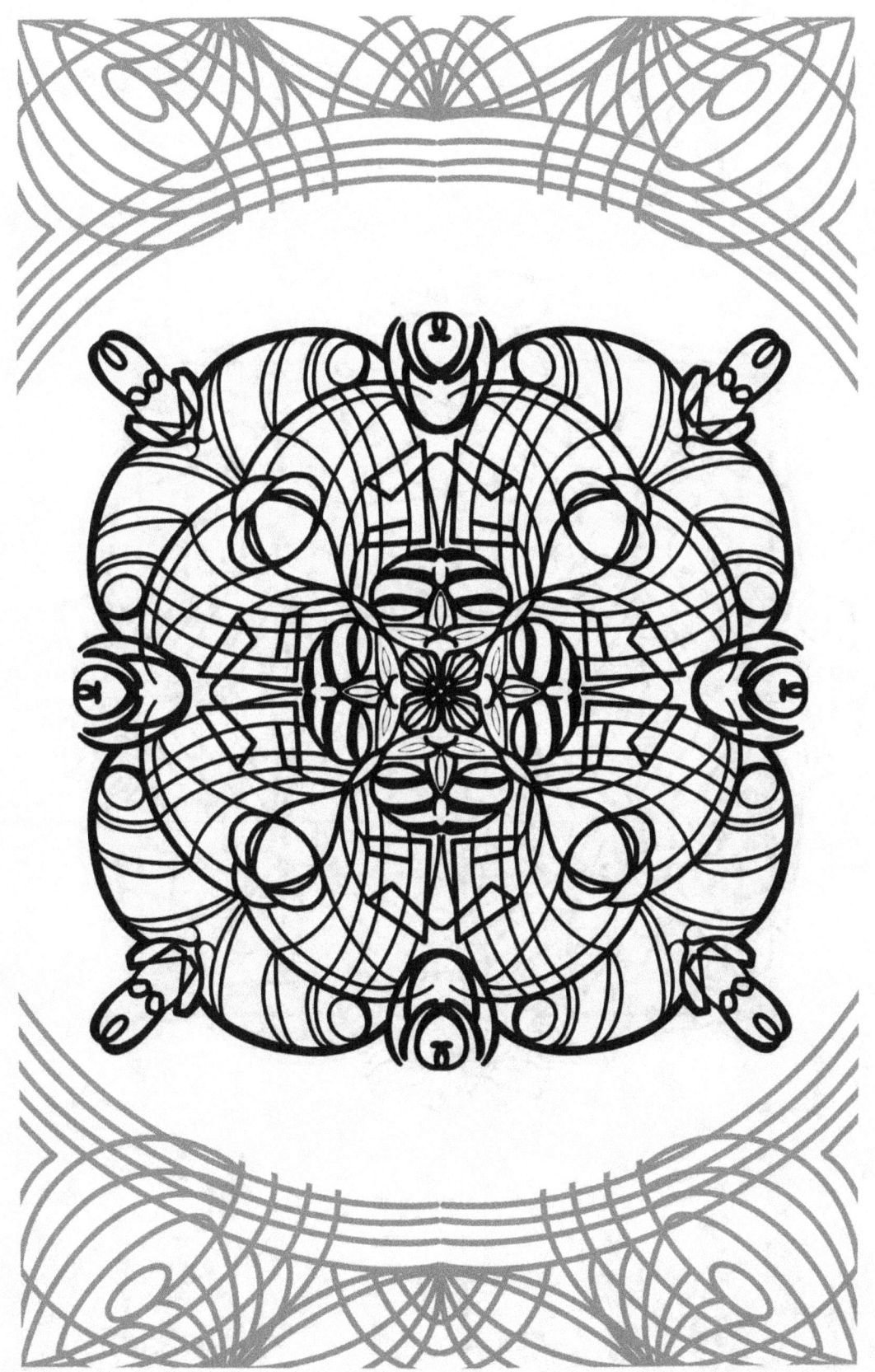

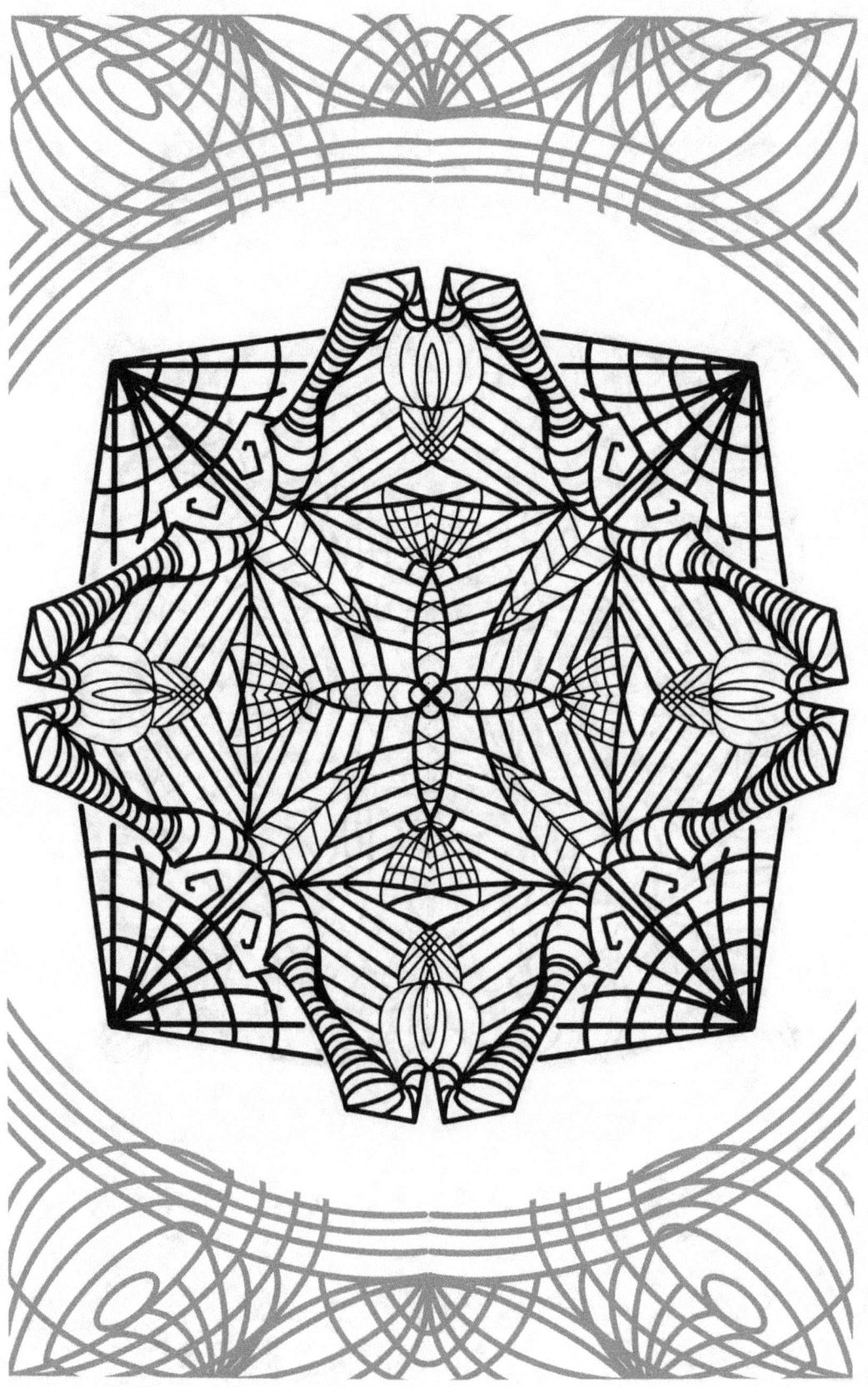

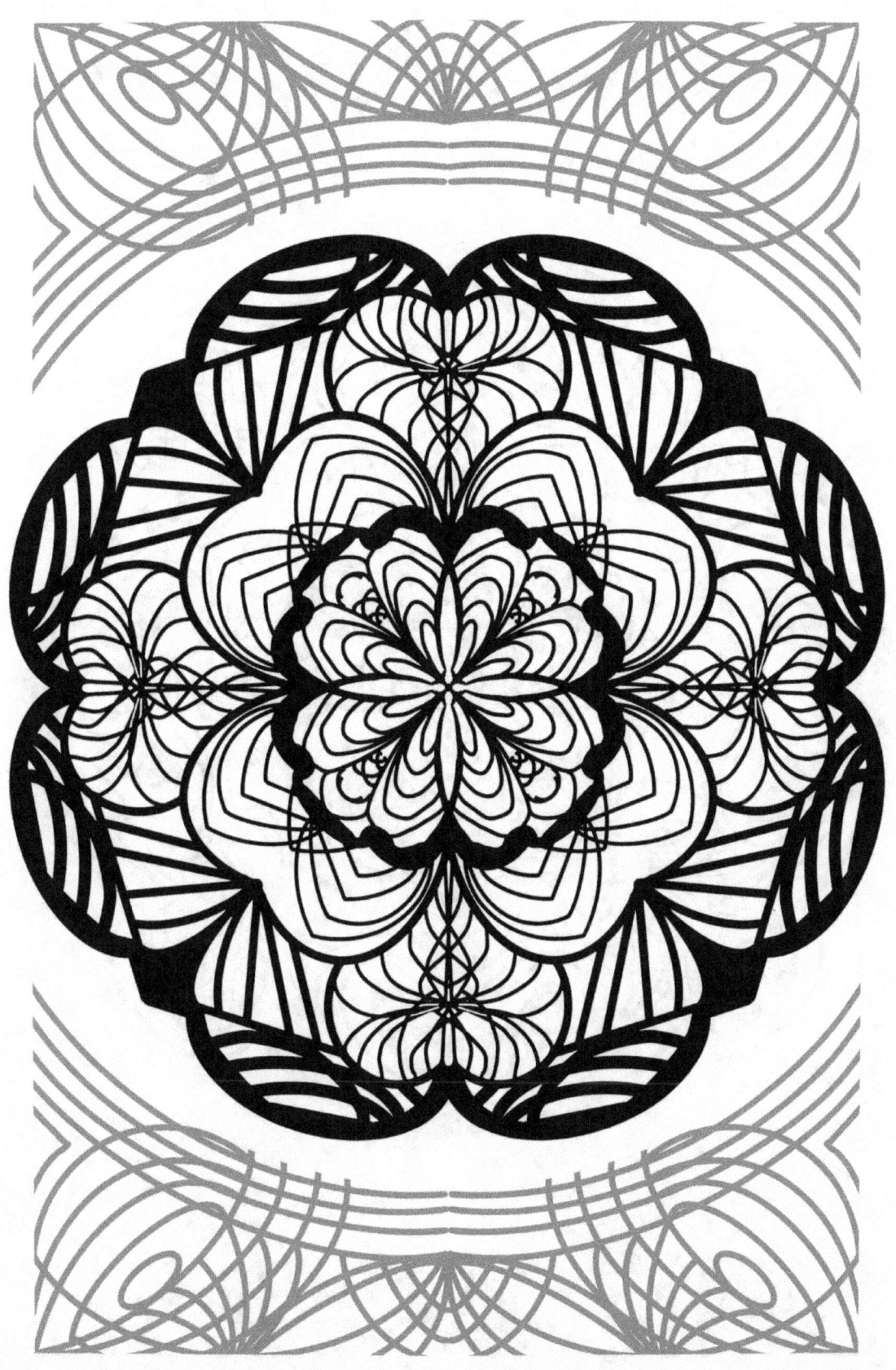

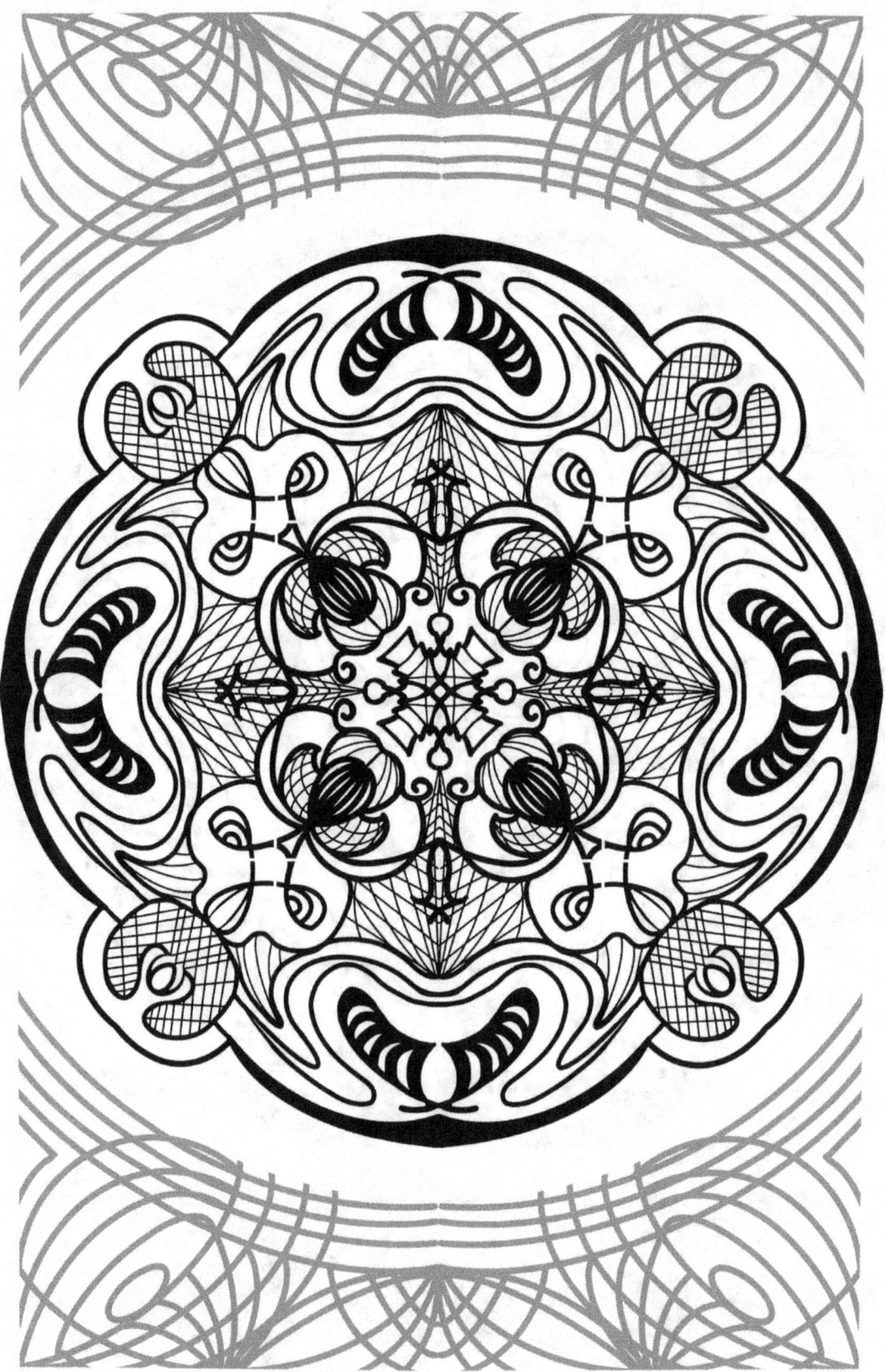

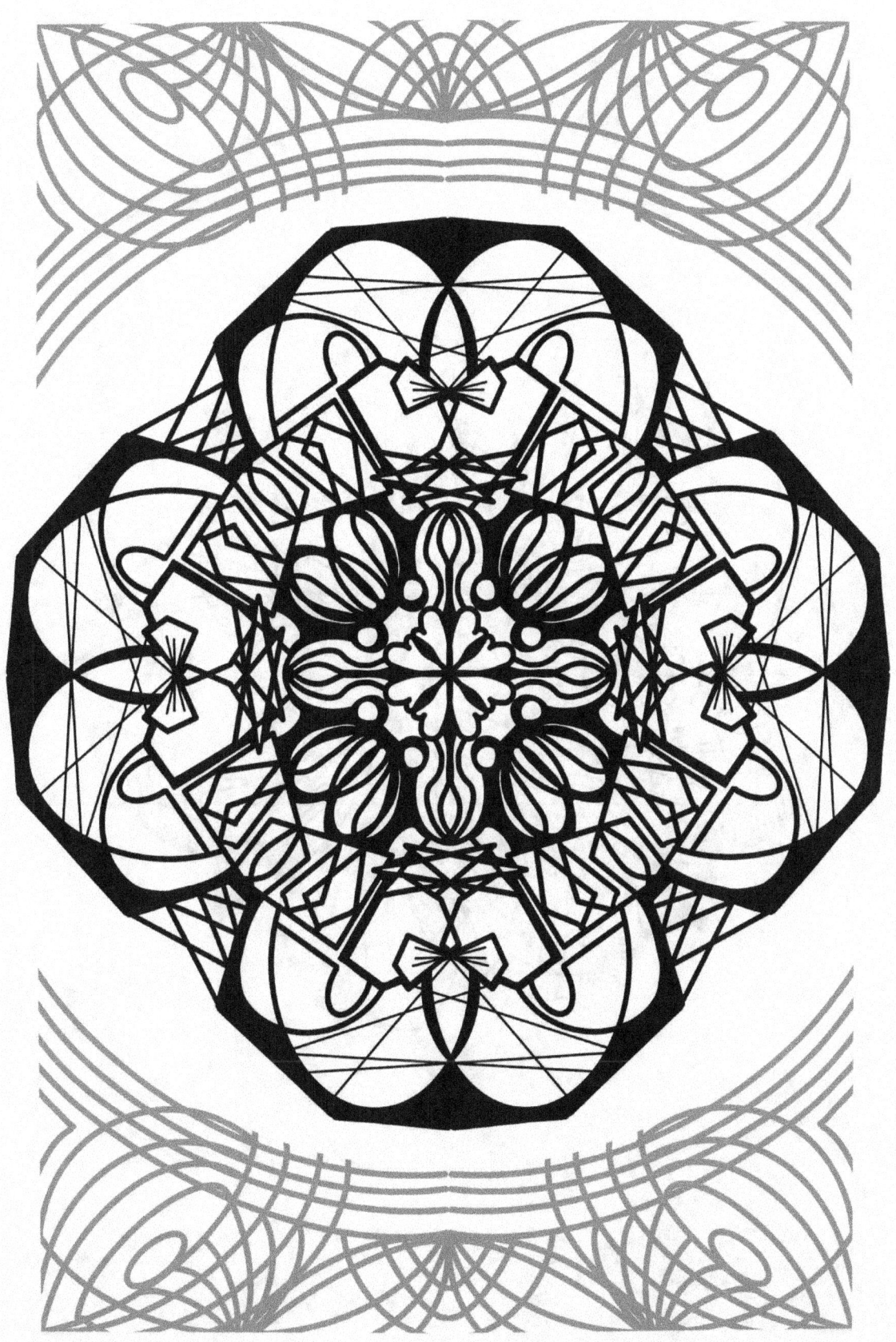

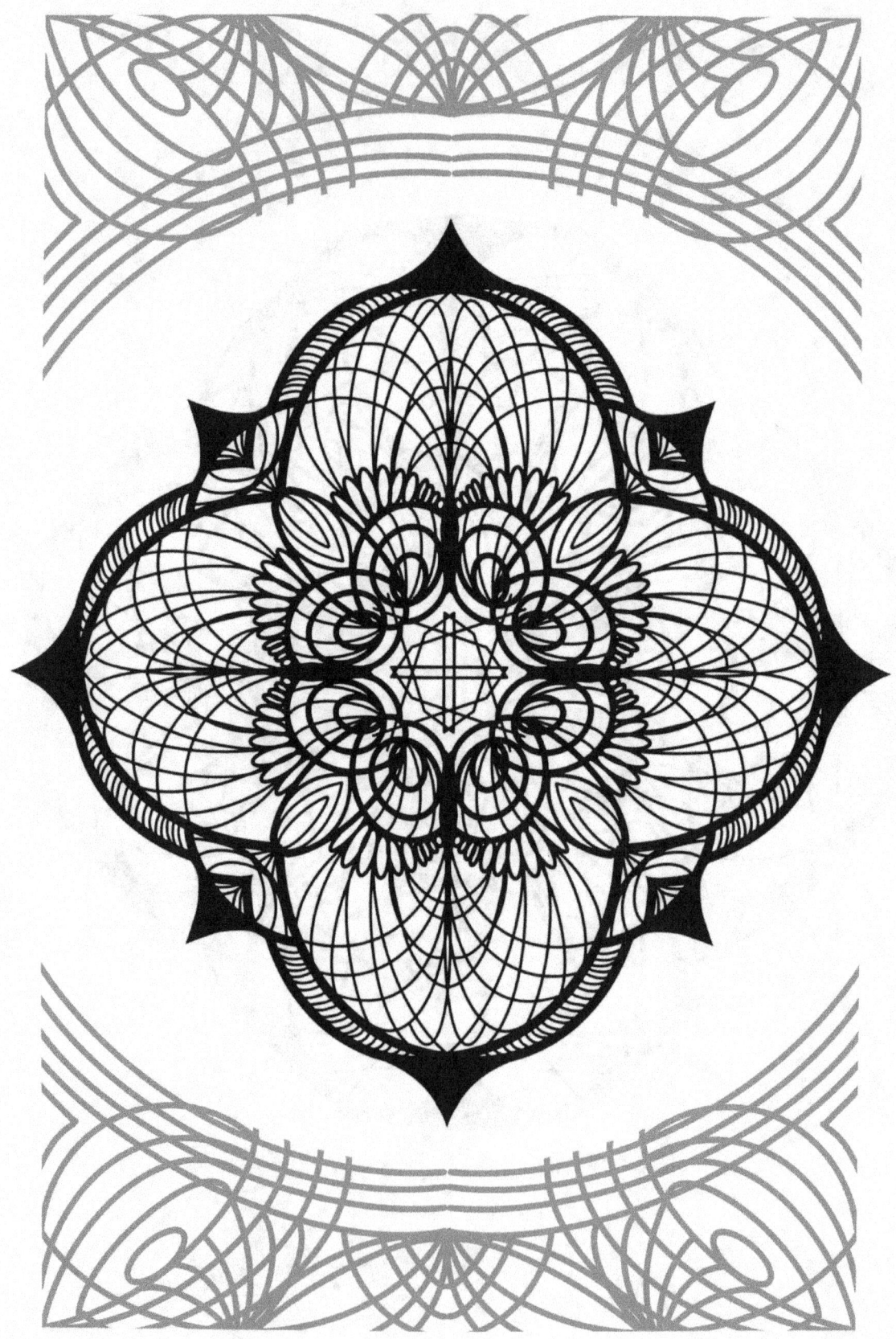

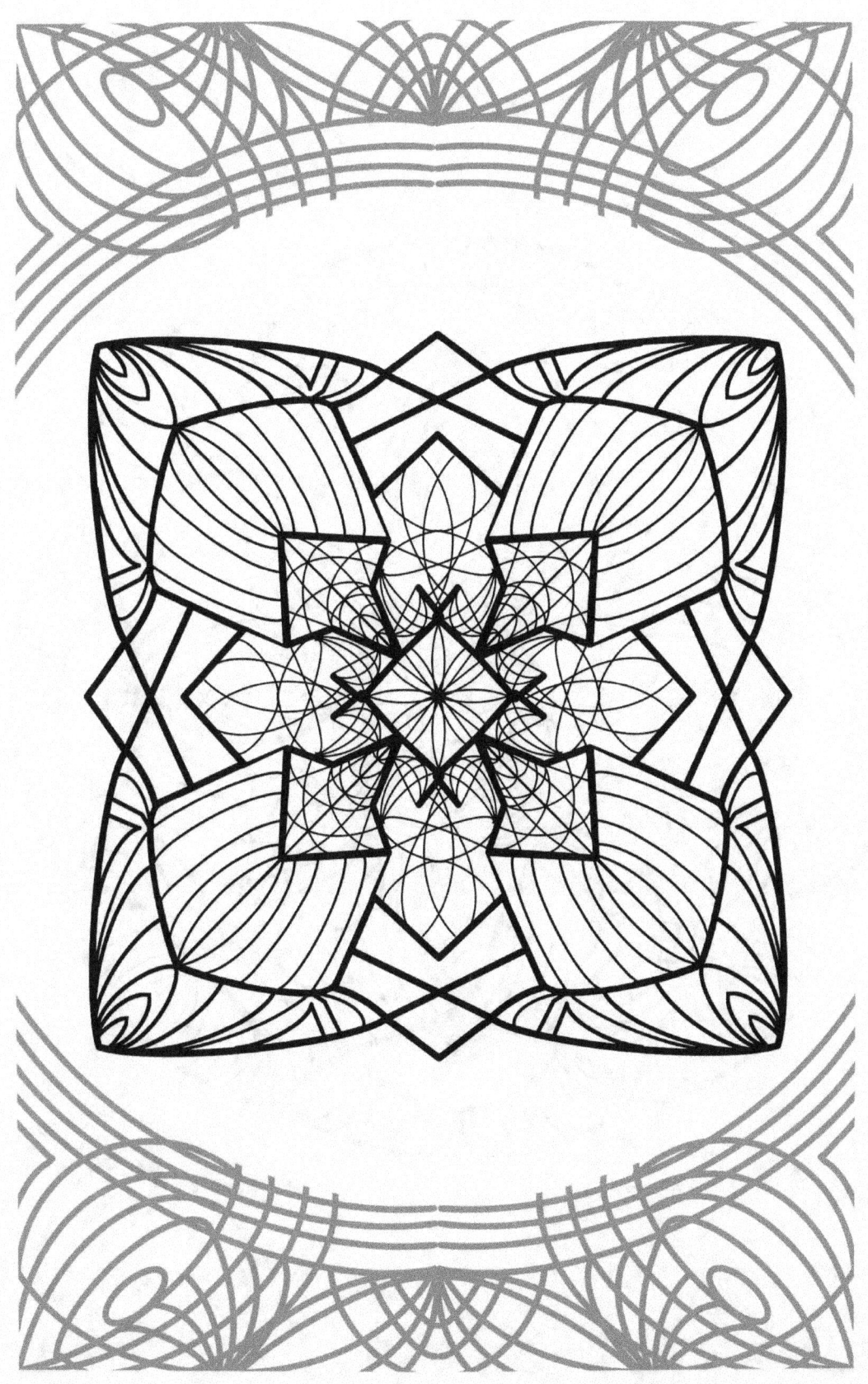

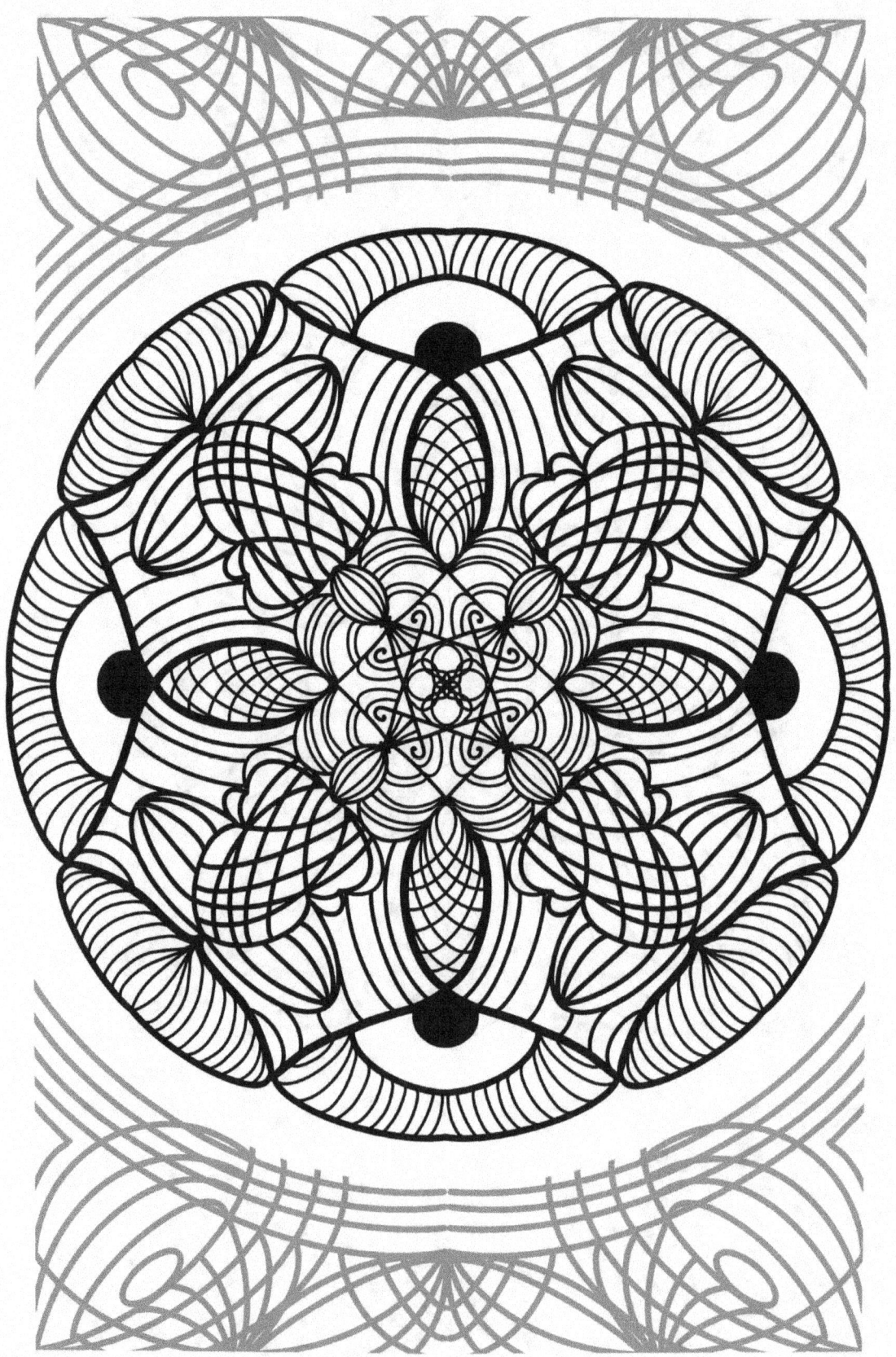

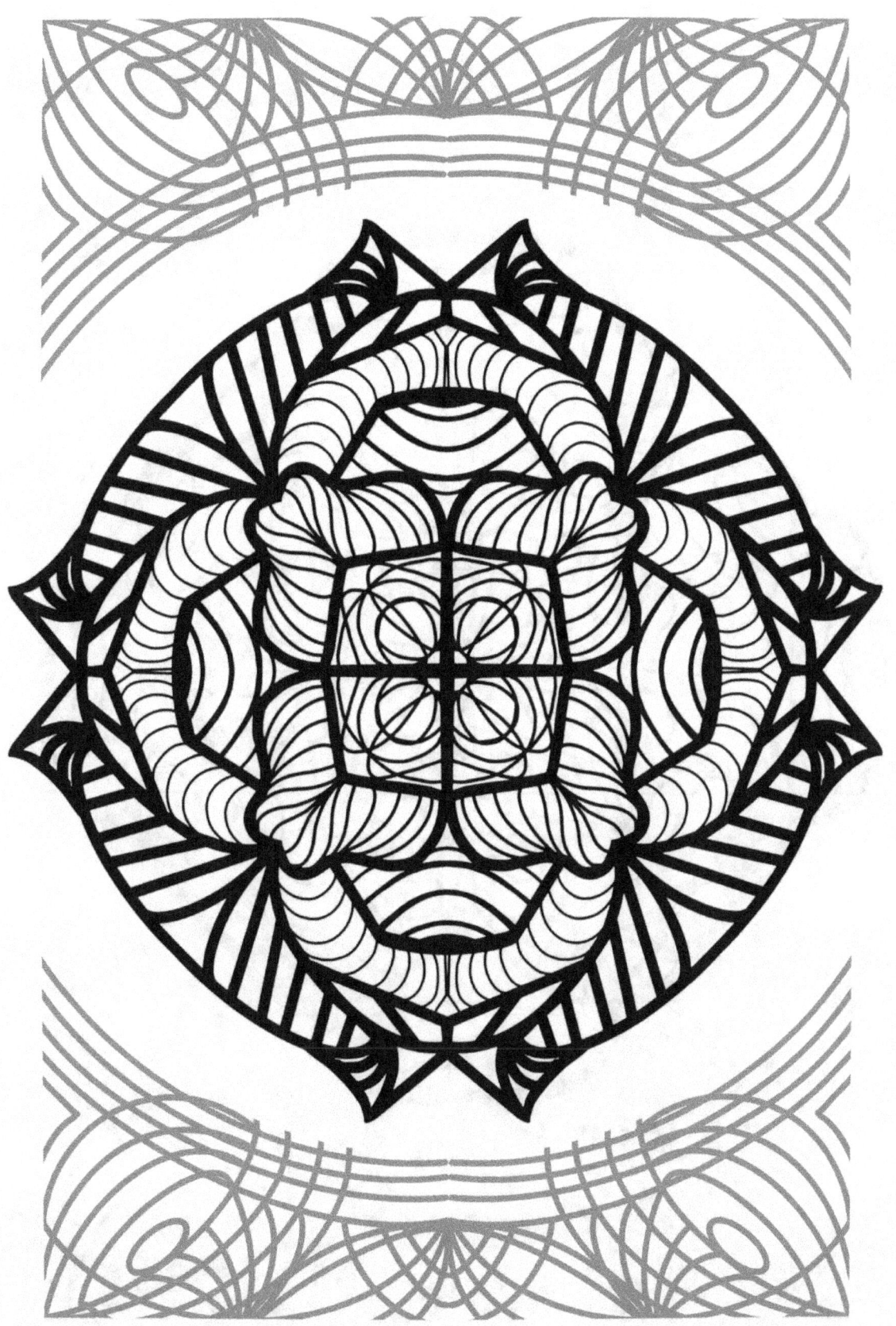

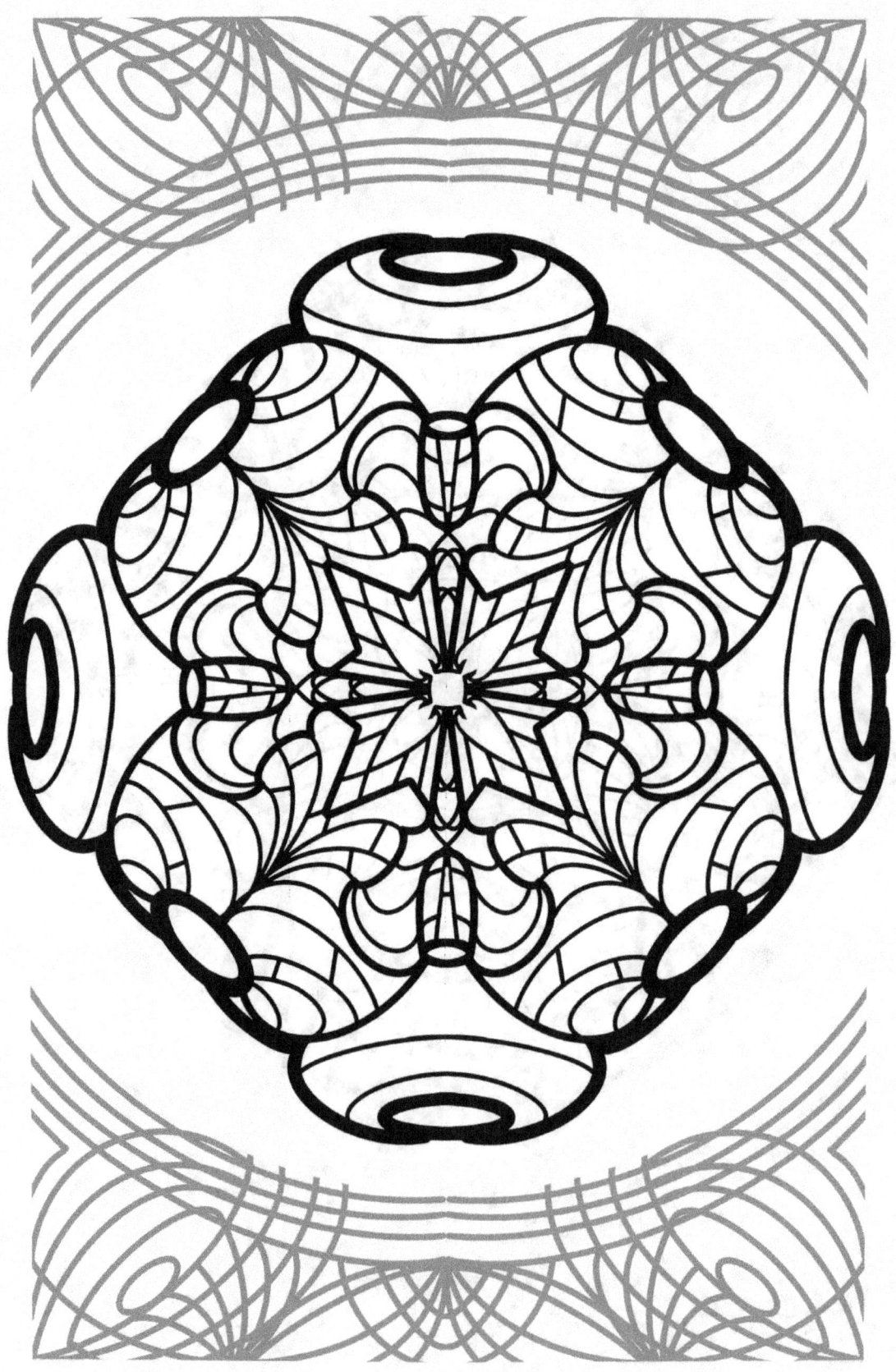

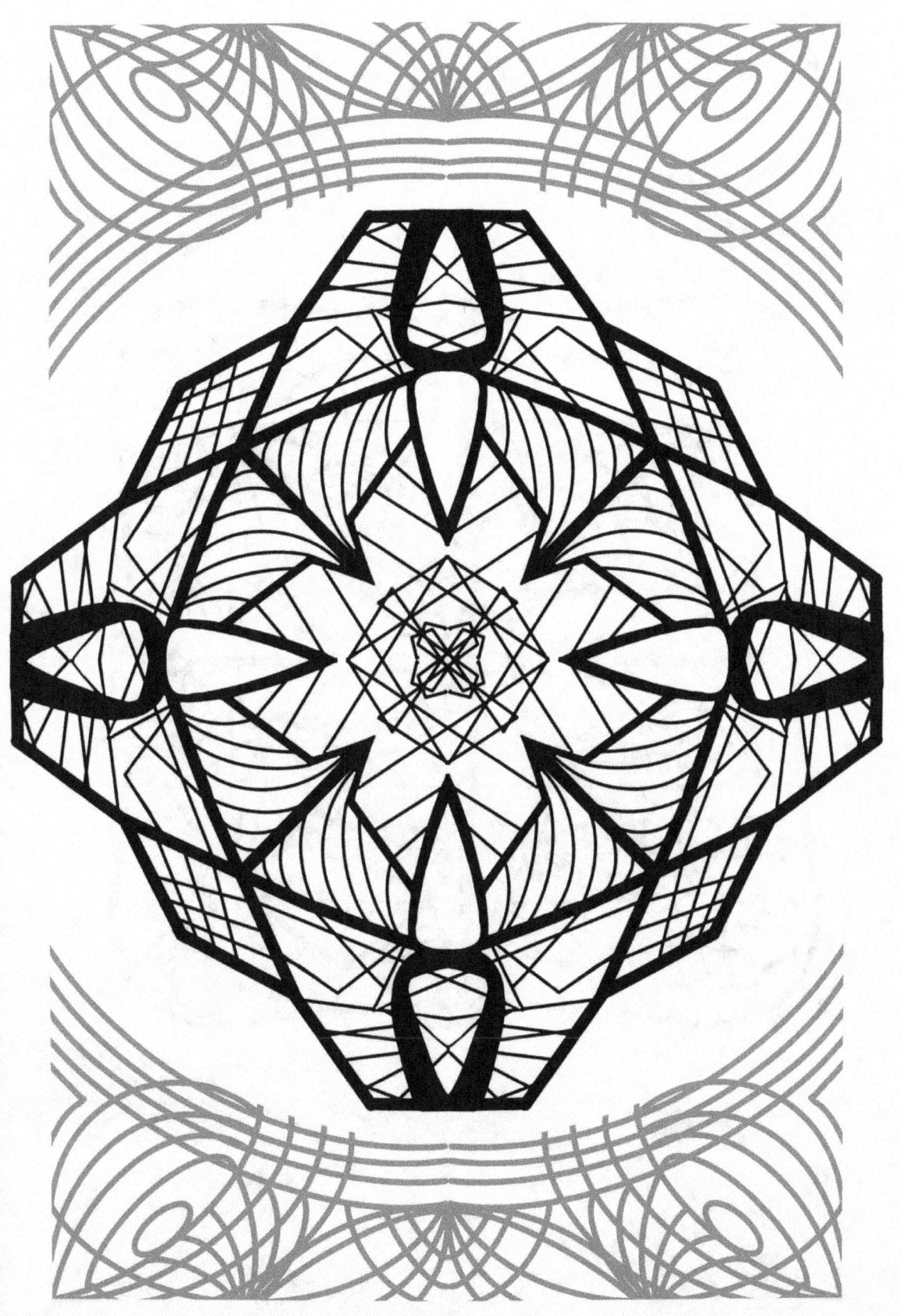

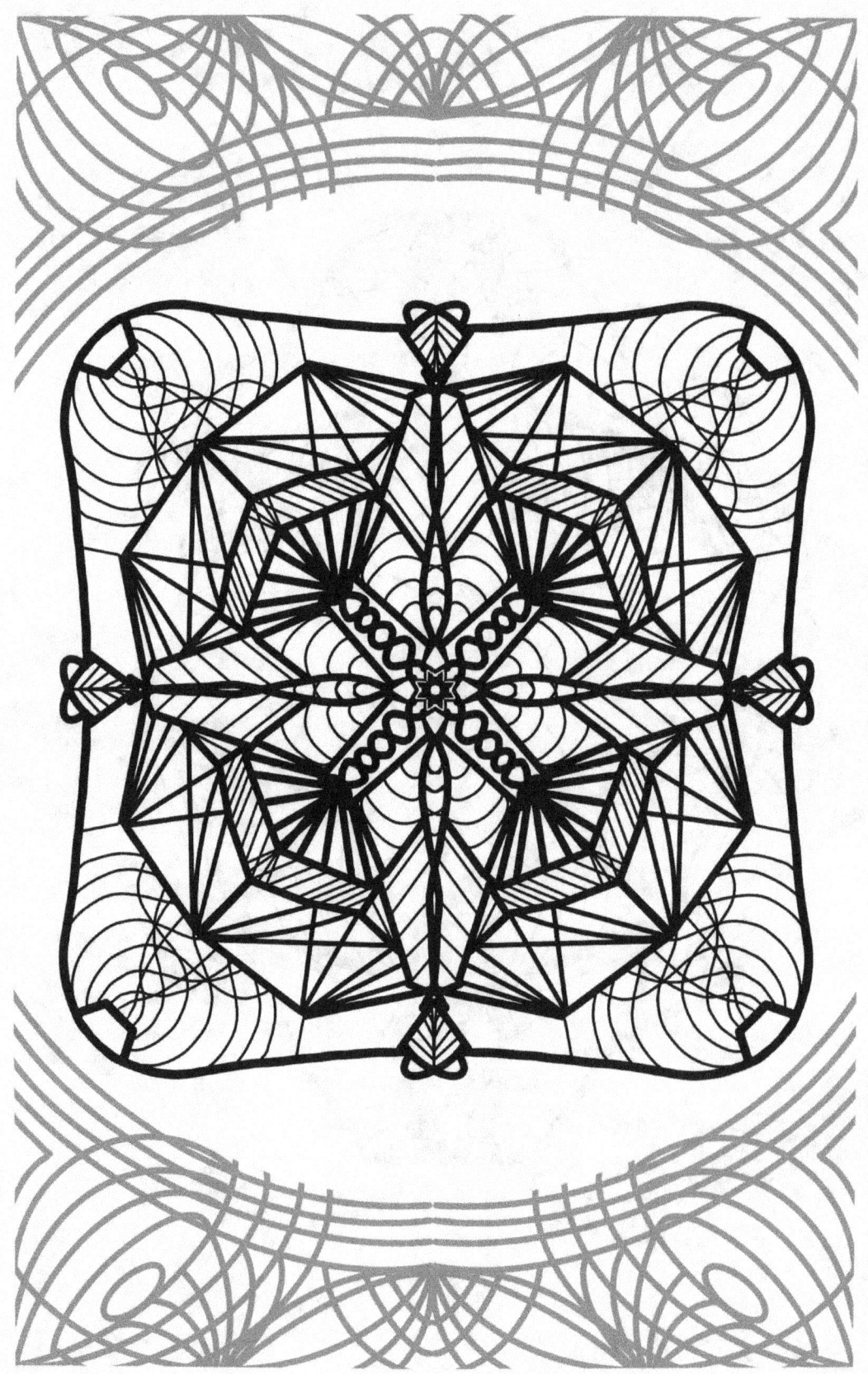

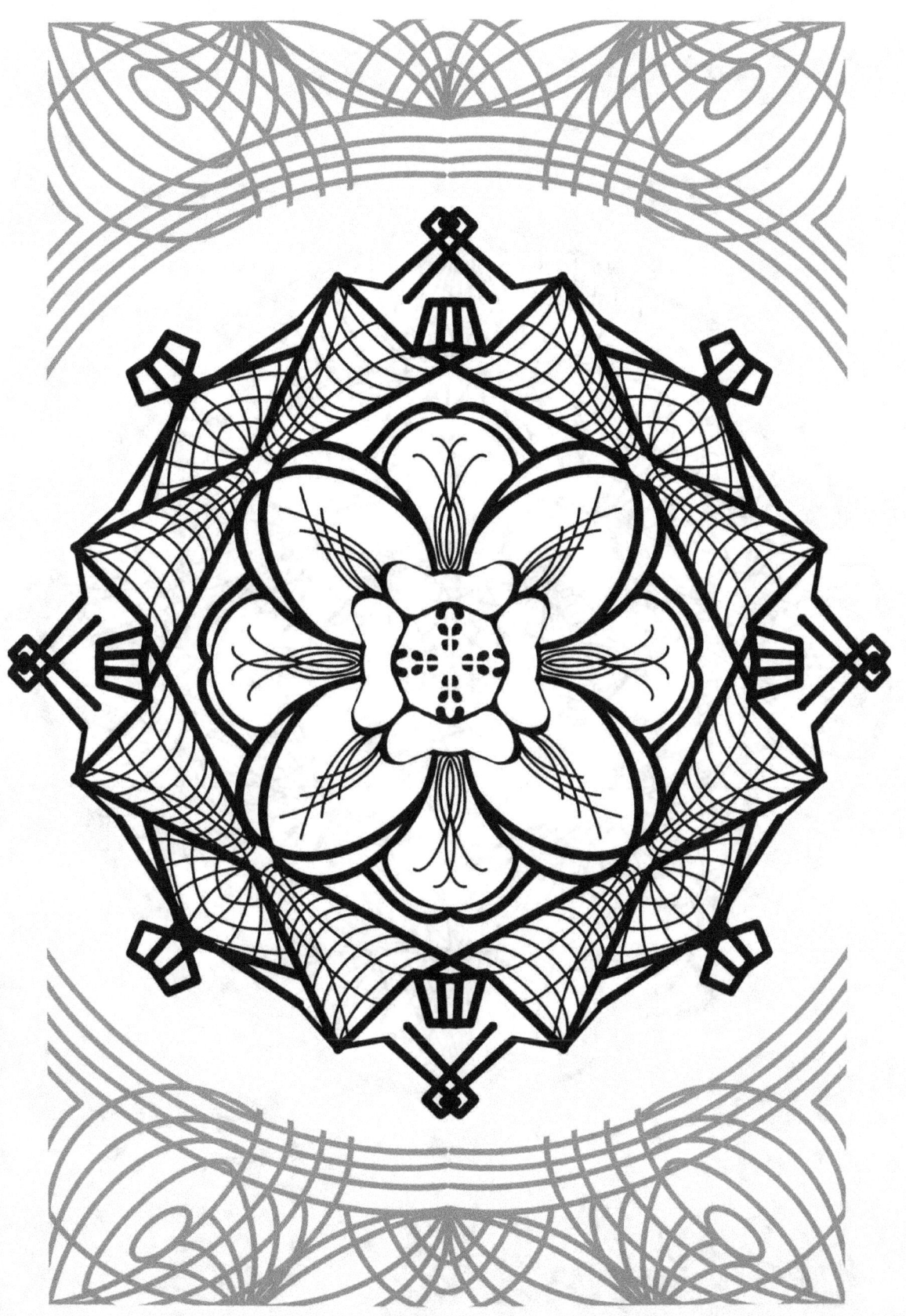

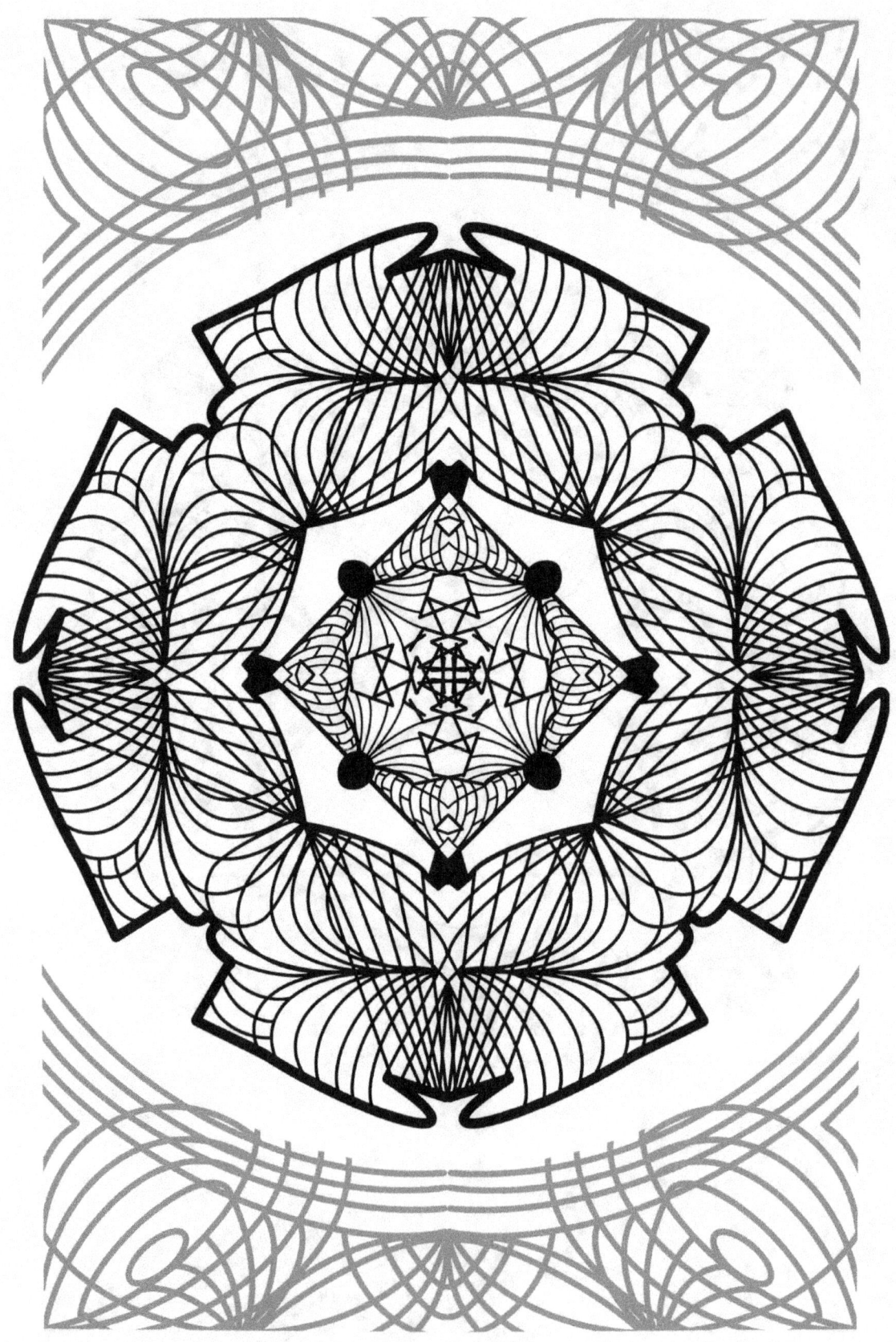

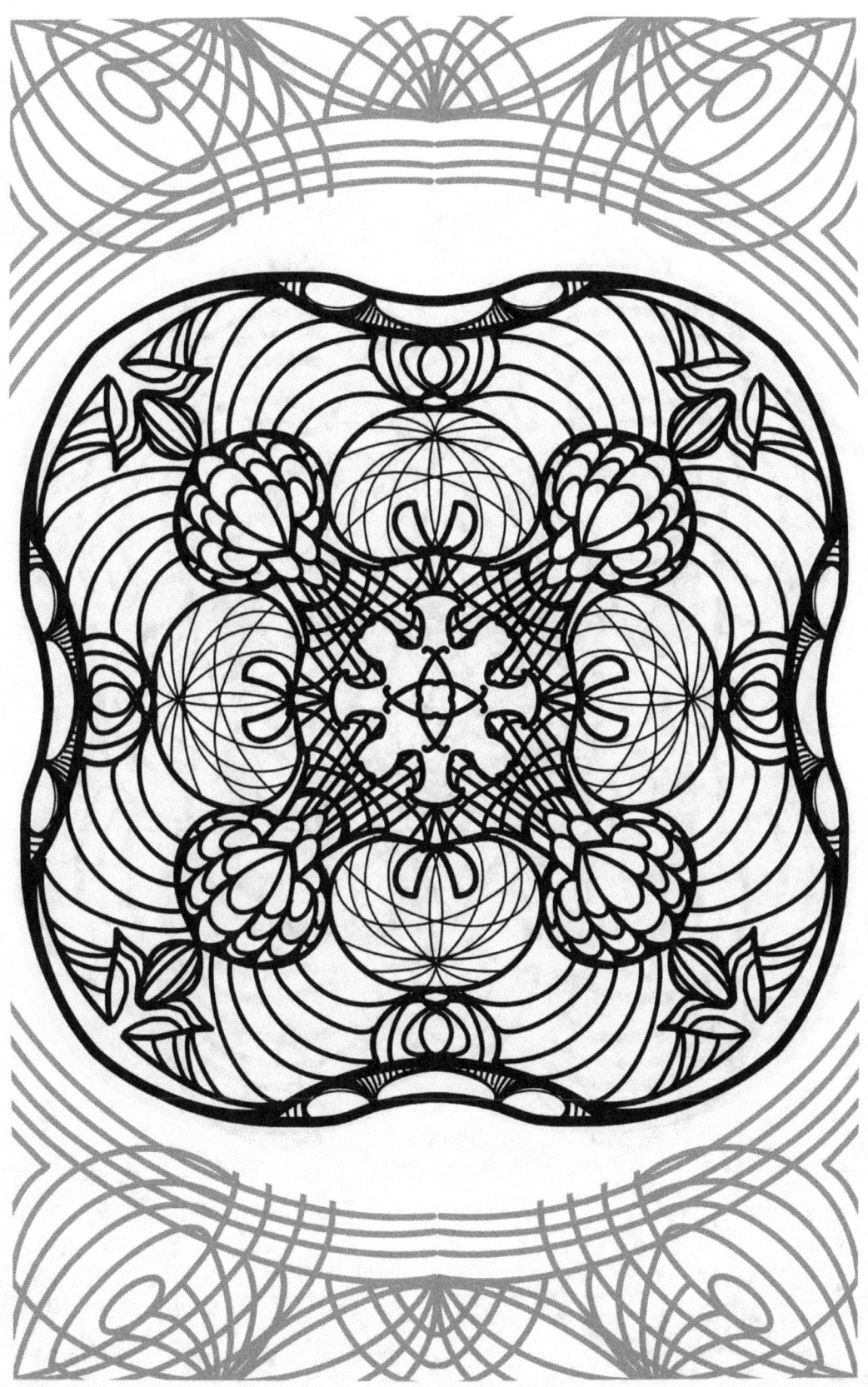

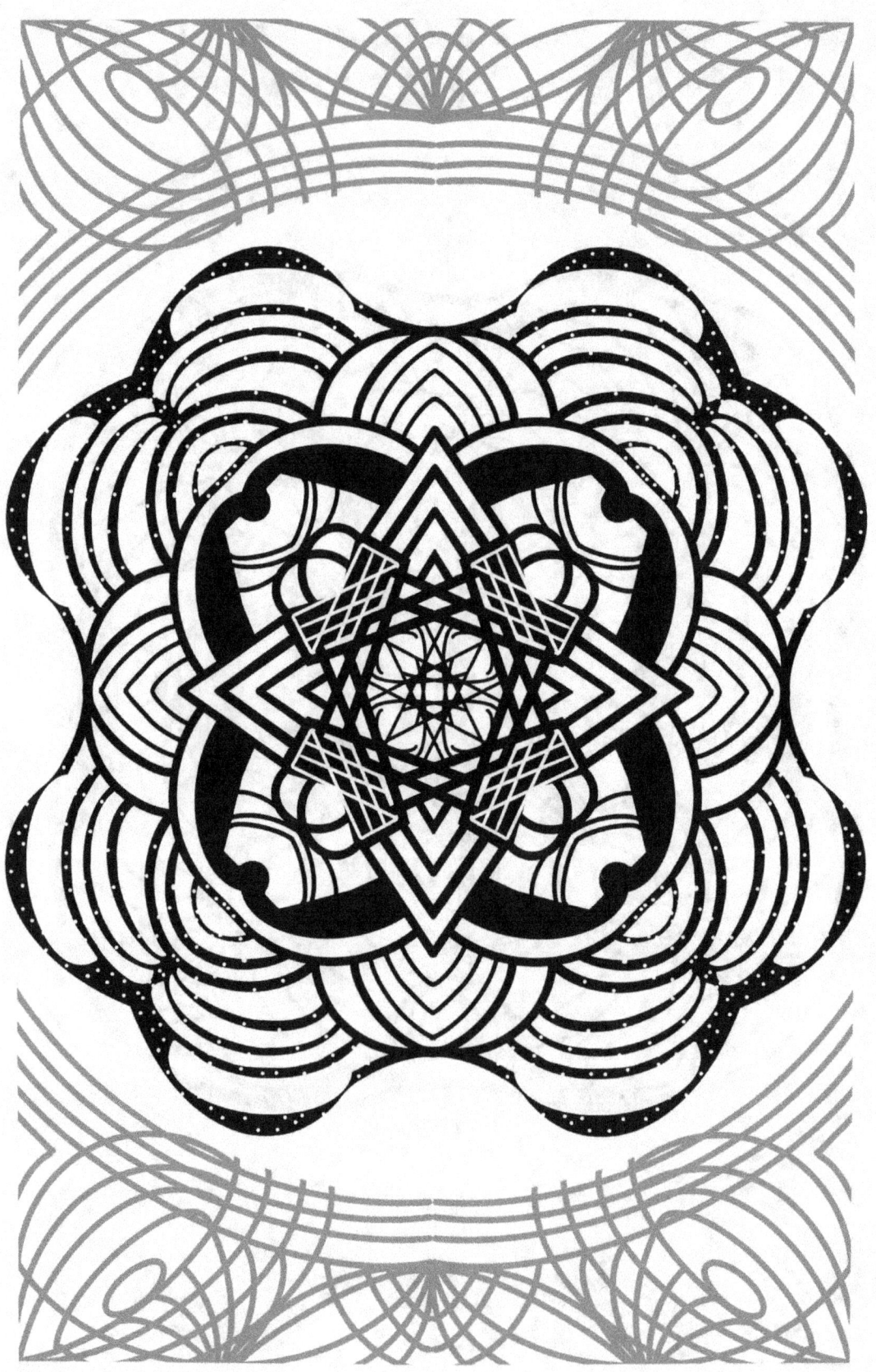

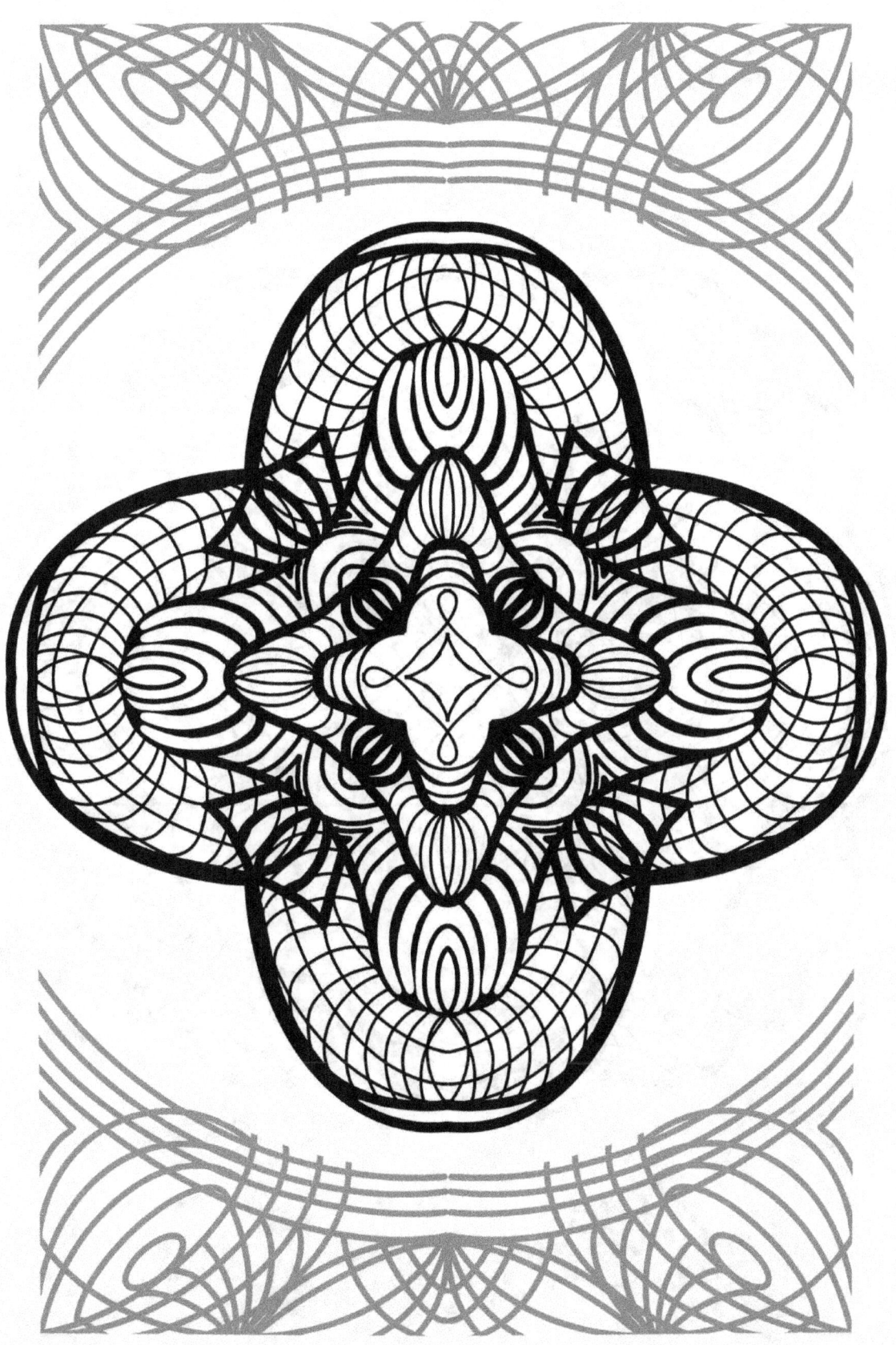

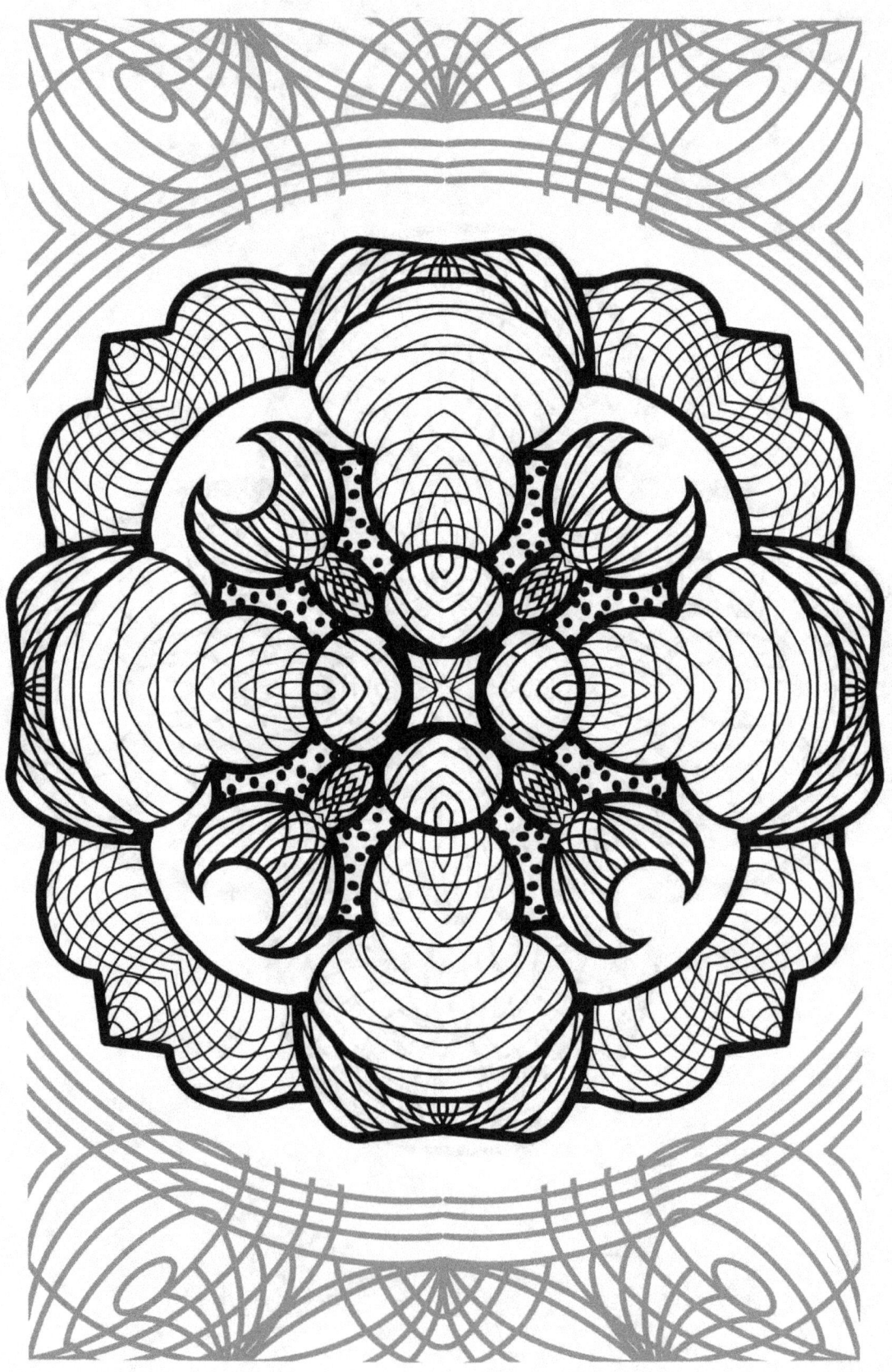

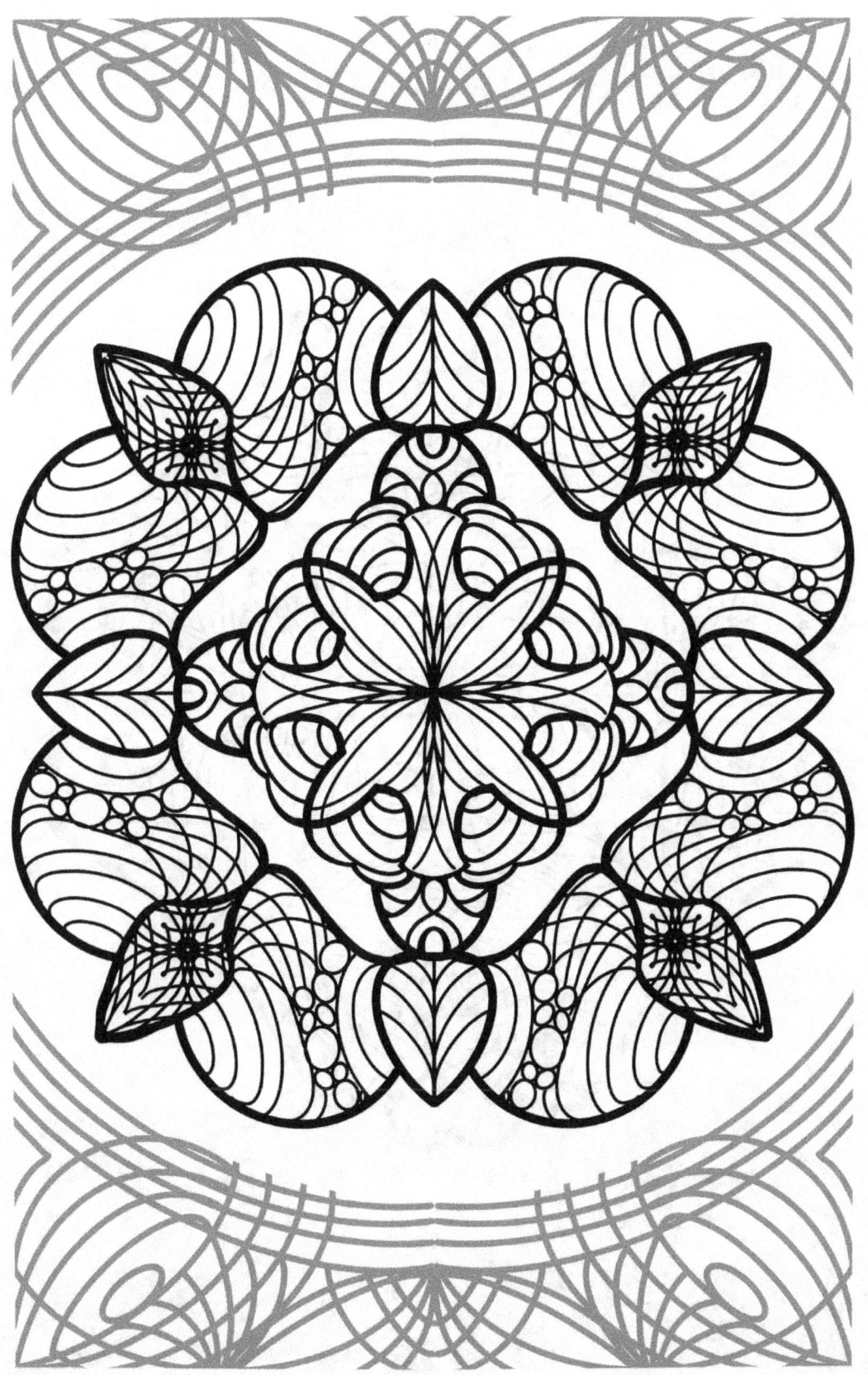

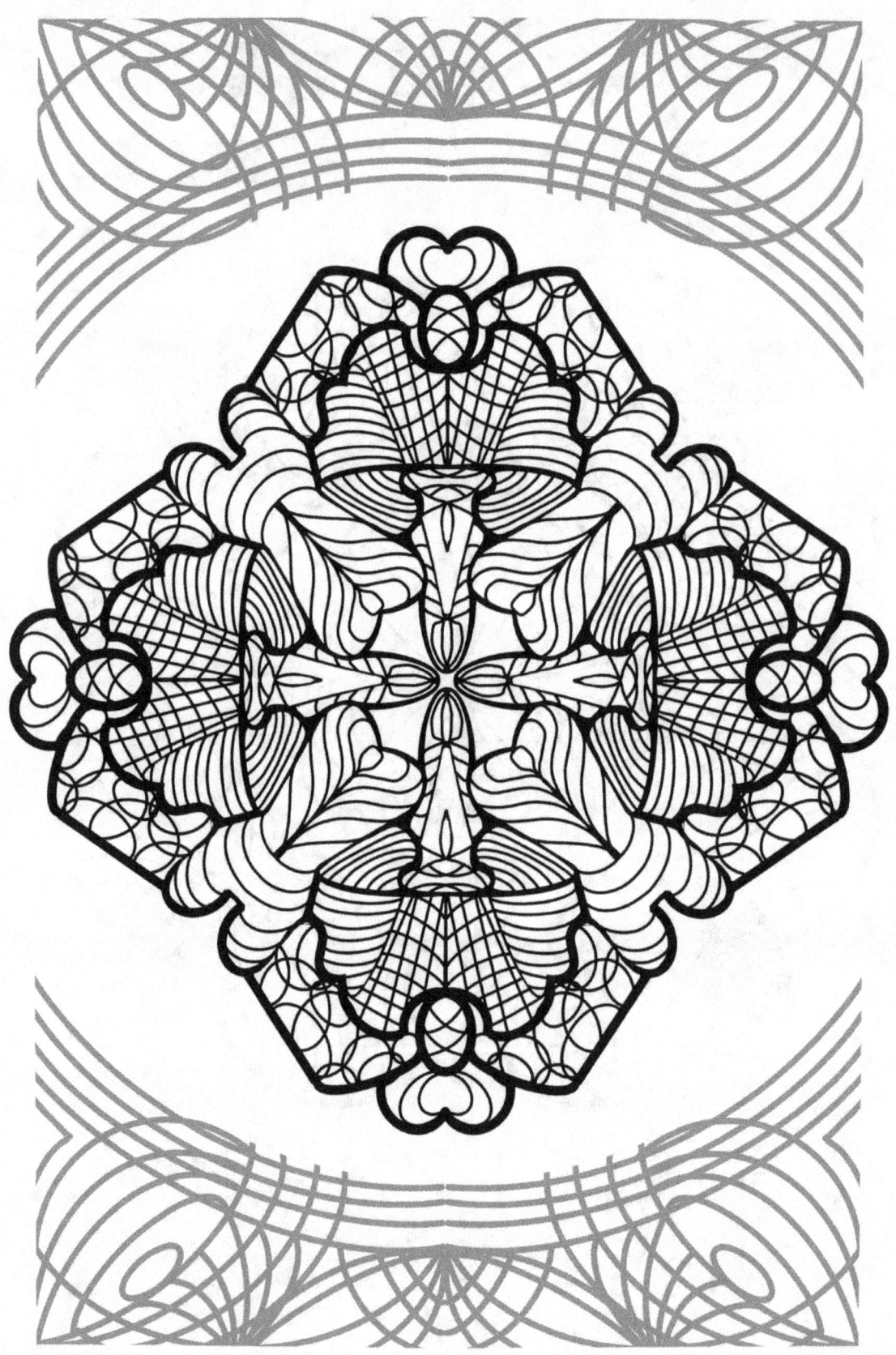

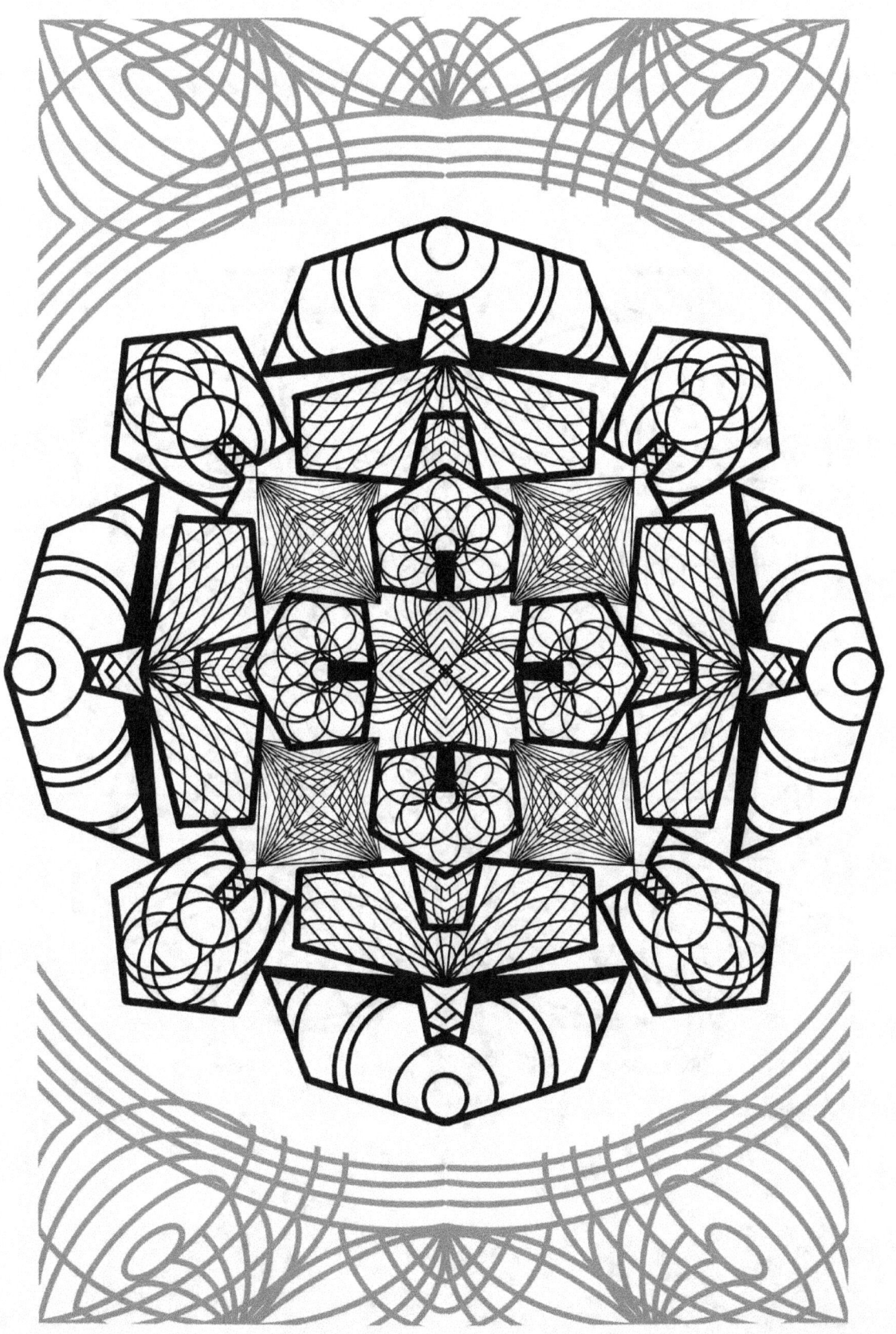

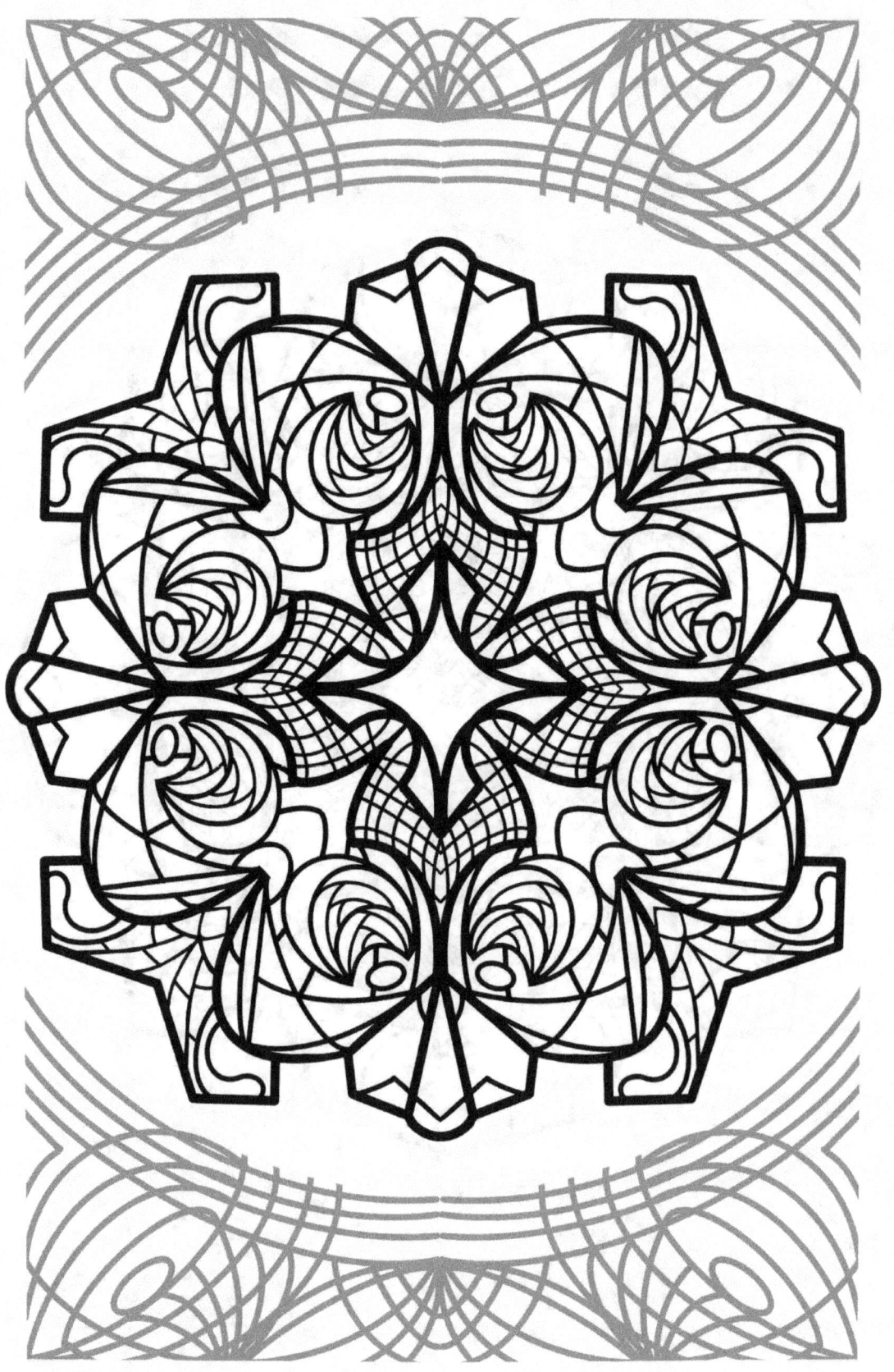

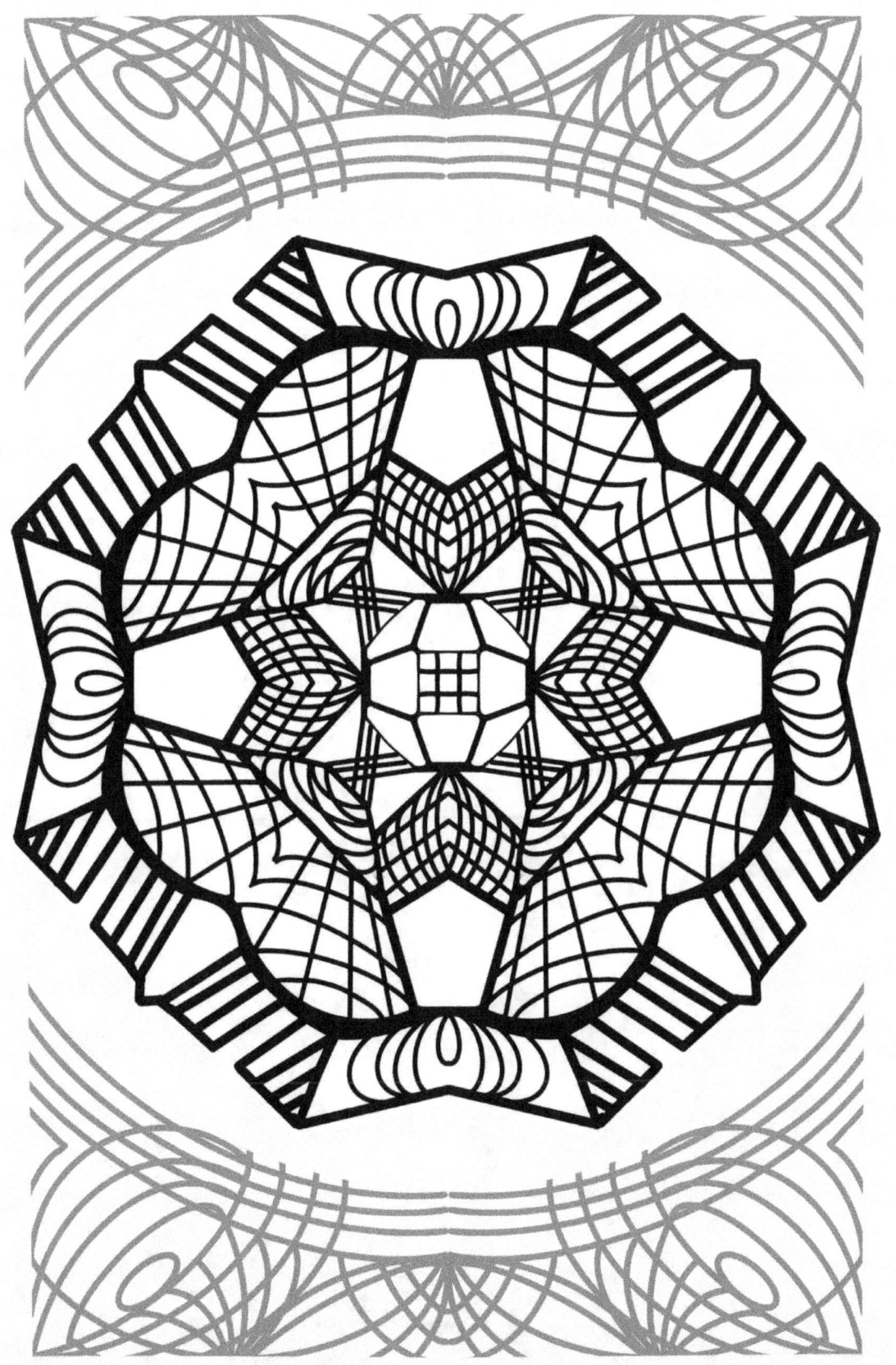

www.ingramcontent.com/pod-product-compliance
Lightning Source LLC
Chambersburg PA
CBHW081531220526
45467CB00010B/3121